Schriften zum geistigen Eigentum
und zum Wettbewerbsrecht

Herausgegeben von

Prof. Dr. Christian Berger, Universität Leipzig
Prof. Dr. Horst-Peter Götting, Techn. Universität Dresden

Band 34

Horst-Peter Götting/Michał du Vall (†)/
Heike Röder-Hitschke (Hrsg.)

Enforcing Intellectual Property Rights

Necessary Instruments versus Over-Enforcement

Nomos

Die Deutsche Nationalbibliothek verzeichnet diese Publikation in der Deutschen Nationalbibliografie; detaillierte bibliografische Daten sind im Internet über http://dnb.d-nb.de abrufbar.

ISBN 978-3-8329-5366-9

1. Auflage 2012

in memoriam Michał du Vall

Preface

The enforcement of intellectual property rights has been one of the most important and controversial issues for almost a decade now. In order to achieve at least a minimum harmonization within the European Union, the widely debated Directive 2004/48/EC on the enforcement of intellectual property rights should provide uniform measures to be adopted by the member states. More than two years after the implementation of this so-called Enforcement-Directive into Polish Law and about one year after its implementation into German Law, members of the Institute for Intellectual Property, Competition and Media Law (IGEWeM) at the Technische Universität Dresden and the Institute of Intellectual Property Law at the Uniwersytet Jagielloński in Kraków discussed the impact of these (in part) new legal standards on national law and proceedings and the question if the reinforced recognition of intellectual property rights has reached its limits, in a bilateral conference.

This conference on "Enforcing Intellectual Property Rights - Necessary Instruments versus Over-Enforcement", organized by the IGEWeM Dresden in cooperation with the Institute of Intellectual Property Law, was held on 9 and 10 October 2009 in Dresden. Being the second conference of its kind, it followed a tradition of regular scientific exchange and conferences on current issues in intellectual property law between both institutes. This tradition was first established in 2007 with a conference on "Recent Developments in IP Law - European, German and Polish Perspective", organized by the Institute of Intellectual Property Law in Kraków.

Eleven speakers participated in this conference and contributed to an intense and fruitful discussion on civil enforcement, actual problems of competition law and objections and counterclaims in IP-Litigation. Our special thanks go to the speakers and authors who made the conference as well as this publication possible. Even if some time has passed since then, their conference contributions are still relevant today and almost all of them could be put together in this volume.

A third bilateral conference is planned for autumn 2012 and will probably take place in Kraków.

Dresden / Kraków, in December 2011

Prof. Dr. Horst Peter Götting
Prof. Dr. Michał du Vall
Heike Röder-Hitschke

Contents

Implementation of the Enforcement Directive into Polish Law - Substantive Law Aspects

Anna Tischner

I. Introduction

It is unquestionable that the protection of intellectual property constitutes the area of law in which the European legislator is very active. However, the results of this activity need to be implemented into national laws in a way which is congruent with the intended goals and does not destroy legal systems of the EU member states too much. More than three years after the deadline for implementation of the directive 2004/48/EC of 29 April 2004 on the enforcement of intellectual property rights[1] into the national legal orders constitutes a good time perspective to assess the real need of this act, its value and effects on the improvement of the protection of these rights in EU member states (i.e. the real enforcement which was to be enhanced by this act). It should be pointed out that the Enforcement Directive, adopted on the eve of admitting ten new members of the EU in 2004, is perceived as the demonstration of will of the European policy-makers[2] and vote of no confidence in the efficiency of the protection of intellectual property in these countries. The results of this improvement made as a last-minute attempt will be discussed on the example of Polish law.

The main feature of the regulation of liability for the infringements of the intellectual property rights in Poland is that each specific act in this area of law has its own catalogue of claims in case of an infringement. This kind of regulation arose with the historical development of Polish intellectual property law since most of the specific regulations were drafted before the adoption of the general regulation of the Polish civil law. To limit the doubts as to the scope of liability in case of infringement a separate catalogue of claims was included in each specific act. Unfortunately, the legislator did not care about the coherence between these regulations. This legislation technique is nowadays well established in Polish law, also despite the existence of the general regulation of civil law – the

1 OJ EU L 157 of 30 April 2004, p. 45; corrected version: OJ EU L 195 of 2 June 2004, p. 16 (hereinafter the "Directive"). According to Art. 20 of the Directive member states were obligated to bring into force the laws and other regulations necessary to comply with the Directive by 29 April 2006.

2 A. Kur, *The Enforcement Directive – Rough Start, Happy Landing?*, 35 IIC 821 (2004).

Civil Code, which should be a keystone for all the area of private law. Consequently, before the harmonization of the Polish law with the requirements of the Enforcement Directive there existed material discrepancies between the accessible measures in case of the infringement of different intellectual property rights. However, the implementation of the Enforcement Directive increased these differences and incoherencies.

The act implementing the Directive into Polish law[3] came into force on 20 June 2007. This act harmonized regulations of civil measures in case of infringement of several intellectual property rights: copyright and related rights, *sui generis* rights to a database, rights to the topography of a semiconductor product, trademark rights, design rights, patent rights, rights to geographical indications, utility model rights and plant variety rights. To this end several specific acts regulating different subject matters of intellectual property law were amended. The Polish legislator decided to exclude unfair competition law from the process of implementation even though certain areas of intellectual property are protected indirectly by the Unfair Competition Act[4]. Obviously, it is not a mistake taking into account the provisions of the Enforcement Directive[5] but in Poland the Unfair Competition Act is in practice very often used as a legal ground to protect intellectual property (e.g. unregistered trade mark, trade name). Consequently, this decision spoils the cohesion of the system. Namely, before the implementation of the Enforcement Directive the catalogue of claims provided for in the Unfair Competition Act and in other acts protecting specific subject matters of intellectual property was comparable, regardless of the delictual nature of protection against unfair competition acts.

Currently, the differences between the available measures are so significant that it may be perceived as a manifestation of the imbalance in the protection of intellectual property. It is even more visible when we compare the catalogues of claims in each act regulating the specific subject matter of intellectual property. The Polish legislator, for some unknown reason, provided for material differences in these catalogues of claims (e.g. the scope of claims for damages and recovery of profits). As a result of the harmonization of Polish law with the European standards outlined in the Directive we have different levels of protection as regards the available claims depending on their legal basis. Consequently, im-

3 Act of 9 May 2007 amending the Act on copyright and related rights and several other acts, Polish OJ of 2007, No. 99, para. 662.

4 Act on suppression of unfair competition of 16 April 1993, consolidated text: Polish OJ of 2003, No. 153, para. 1503 amended (hereinafter the "Unfair Competition Act").

5 See recital 13 of the Directive's preamble and the Statement by the Commission concerning Art. 2 of Directive 2004/48/EC of the European Parliament and of the Council on the enforcement of intellectual property rights (2005/295/EC), OJ EU L 94 of 13 April 2005, p. 37.

proving enforcement of intellectual property resulted in differentiating individual rights and claims available in case of their infringement.

In April 2009 the Polish Ministry of Culture and National Heritage prepared, pursuant to the requirements of Art. 18 of the Directive, a report on the implementation of this Act.[6] In the general assessment included in the Report it is clearly stated that the amendment of Polish law due to the requirements of the Directive has little influence on the level of innovative activities and development of the information society. Moreover, the consulted entities have better assessed the legal solutions which were in force before implementation of the Directive. In the Report it is also criticized that the implementation of the Directive in Poland caused different levels of protection of individual intellectual property rights.

II. The scope of harmonization – combating piracy v. prevention of any infringement of IP

The main goal of the proposal of the Directive[7] was to enhance the level of protection of intellectual property rights across the European Union in order to combat piracy and counterfeiting. Special attention should be drawn to the fact that the primary aim of the act was not to combat any infringement of these rights but it was planned to refer only to infringements carried out for commercial purposes or causing significant harm to the right holder. Finally, according to Art. 2 Sec. 1 of the Directive it applies to any infringement of intellectual property rights. In the preamble to the Directive there is an extensive discussion of the necessity to ensure that the substantive law on intellectual property is applied effectively in the Community, as the means of enforcing intellectual property rights are of paramount importance for the success of the internal market.

This significant change of mind of the European legislator was criticized on several occasions by prominent academics.[8] As a consequence of this change, it was necessary to take into account in the harmonization process the rule of proportionality of the provided measures basing on Art. 3 (2) of the Enforcement Directive and recital No. 17 of the preamble which calls for taking due account of the specific characteristics of the infringing case, including the specific features of each intellectual property right and, where appropriate, the intentional or

6 In Polish: http://www.mkidn.gov.pl/cps/rde/xbcr/mkid/enforcement_sprawozdanie_przyjete_przez_KERM.pdf (hereinafter the "Report").

7 Proposal of 30 January 2003, Doc. COM (2003) 46 final.

8 W. R. Cornish, J. Drexl, R. Hilty, A. Kur, *Procedures and Remedies for Enforcing IPRs: the European Commission's Proposed Directive*, 2003 EIPR 447.

unintentional character of the infringement, treating these provisions as the last hope. In my opinion the Polish legislator did not make good use of this option which transpires from the discussion of individual solutions below.

The subject-matter of the Directive, seemingly limited to the area of intellectual property, in fact significantly encroaches on the territory of the general civil law and civil procedure. To achieve the outlined aims of the Directive the intervention into national legal orders with regard to civil liability was necessary. It is even said that the Directive constitutes the first step to *de facto* harmonization of civil law in European Union as it strongly relates to liability issues.[9] We may even say that intellectual property law is in the vanguard of the unification of private law in Europe. The main objection that can be raised is that the new Community rules of liability and procedure which relate to the very narrow group of goods are to be included in the national universal regulations, having a long tradition.[10] The conclusions from this method of harmonization are far from optimistic.

III. Particular measures of liability

1. Payment of damages

In Art. 13 of the Enforcement Directive the European legislator made a risky attempt to regulate the uniform minimal standards of the compensation of damages. Doing so he opened Pandora's box. As a result, certain general questions should have been answered: What is the function of compensating damages in European continental law? Is it compensation or prevention? Do we tolerate punitive damages? What do we mean by it? May the payment of damages go beyond the restitution? The provisions of Art. 13 (1 a) of the Directive seem to confirm the general rules of civil liability (with an exception of including infringer's profits – see below III. 2). More problematic is the interpretation and implementation of Art. 13 (1 b) of the Enforcement Directive which alternatively provides for setting the damages as a lump sum on the basis of elements such as at least the amount of royalties or fees which would have been due if the infringer had requested authorization to use the intellectual property right in ques-

9 M. Leistner, *Die „Trojanischen Pferde" der Kommission. Einige Überlegungen zur Entwicklung des allgemeinen Gemeinschaftsprivatrechts vor dem Hintergrund der Harmonisierung des Lauterkeitsrechts und des Rechts des Geistigen Eigentums*, in: *Festschrift für G. Schricker zum 70. Geburtstag*, p. 101 (Munich 2005).

10 W. R. Cornish, J. Drexl, R. Hilty, A. Kur (*supra* note 8), p. 448.

tion. Namely, it is unclear whether the damages in this amount may be set without proving any loss, is this amount minimal and may be multiplied, is it necessary to show the fault of the infringer. With this regards the Directive leaves the national legislator helpless.

As a result of the implementation of the Enforcement Directive into Polish law the compensation of damages was deeply modified. Before the amendment, damages were compensated according to general rules of civil law. Afterwards, the new regulation provided for an option. Namely, according to Art. 296 of the Industrial Property Law in case of an infringement caused by fault, the infringer has to redress the damage in accordance with the general principles of law or by the payment of a sum of money at the amount corresponding to the license fee or of other reasonable compensation, which while being vindicated would have been due on account of consent given by the right holder to exploit his invention.[11] Remarkably, a modified version of this option has been included to the Copyright Act. Under Art. 79 of this Act the infringer of author's economic rights may be obliged to repair the damage on the general terms or by payment of double or, where the infringement is culpable, triple the amount of respective remuneration that would have been due as of the time of claiming it in exchange for the right holder's consent for the use of the work. The latter regulation may be even shocking also when we take into account Anglo-American rules of compensating damages. The Polish legislator did not make use of the optional Art. 13 (2) of the Enforcement Directive which provides for the payment of damages, which may be pre-established.[12]

In my opinion, the correct implementation of Art. 13 of the Directive required to juxtapose this regulation with the national general rules of civil liability. Moreover, the national legislator should have made use of the rule of proportionality (Art. 3 (2) of the Directive) and the prohibition of providing for punitive damages (recital 26). Unfortunately, the Polish legislator ignored all these postulates and the elementary rules of compensating damages, especially the rule *ne quis ex damno suo lucrum faciat* rule. The compensation of damages in copyright law is even more severe than sanctions in criminal law, which are accessible in case of culpable acts. The alternative way of setting damages provokes the question whether in such a case it is necessary to prove the loss, causality and fault of the infringer. We are left with all these elementary questions unanswered. Wasn't it easier to leave the previous regulation untouched? The royalty

11 It is surprising that the amount of the damages should be calculated taking into account the royalty rates due on the day of demanding the compensation and not on the day of infringement. The circumstances may change very much during this period.

12 Such statutory damages were provided in Polish intellectual property law regulations in force before 1939.

rates as an objective indicator of lost profits were well known in the former Polish judicature.

2. Recovery of infringer's profits

The infringement of intellectual property rights often results in the positive changes in the economic situation of the infringer. Namely, as a result of the immaterial nature of these goods, the infringer may reap a profit from the infringed good, even without perceptible loss in the property of the right holder. Moreover, he may save the payment of royalty fees which are due to the right holder in case of the legal exploitation of his rights. All these effects, which we describe as enrichment, may influence positively on the global economic situation of the infringer.

Surprisingly, this aspect of the infringement's effects is mentioned only in Art. 13 (1 a) of the Enforcement Directive, according to which any unfair profits made by the infringer should be taken into account in setting the damages. Such a qualification is very questionable, we can even say – against the rules of compensation for damages in civil law. Moreover, pursuant to Art. 13 (2) of the Directive, in case of innocent infringements (where the infringer did not knowingly, or with reasonable grounds to know, engage in infringing activity) Member States may lay down that the judicial authorities may order the recovery of profits. However, this provision is optional.

There are several measures in the classic civil law which are destined to remove this aspect of illegal activity. First of all, the institution of unjust enrichment should be helpful in such cases. However, in Polish law of intellectual property we may find some misunderstanding as to the function and application of this measure and the scope of recovery in case of unjust enrichment caused by the infringement of immaterial goods. In my opinion, according to the general civil law rule, the claim for recovery of unjust enrichment may be applied in any case of enrichment which has no legal ground, i.e. also in the situation of enrichment caused by the infringement of the intellectual property. Pursuant to the modern theory of this institution[13] and the results of economic analysis of law[14] the claim for recovery of unjust enrichment may be applied in case of any infringement (also innocent, as the fault of the infringer is not a condition of this measure) of the intellectual property right (as it is not limited to the exploitation

13 E. Łętowska, *Bezpodstawne wzbogacenie* (Warszawa 2000); in German literature: E. v. Caemmerer, *Bereicherung und unerlaubte Handlung*, in: *Festschrift für E. Rabel*, Vol. I, p. 353 (Tübingen 1954); R. Ellger, *Bereicherung durch Eingriff* (Tübingen 2002).

14 R. Ellger (*supra* note 13), p. 249.

of the material goods). In case of intellectual property infringements, the scope of liability under this regime is limited to the value of the exploitation of the exclusivity, which usually equals the royalty rates for it. This measure has a corrective function – it should restore the upset balance of property and should have no preventive influence as the character of the infringement (innocent or culpable) has no influence on its application and the scope of recovery.

Nevertheless, these conclusions are not so obvious in the light of present regulations. Pursuant to the regulation of this measure in the Industrial Property Law (Art. 287) the infringer has to return the unlawfully obtained profits, while under the Copyright Act (Art. 79) he is obliged to return the acquired benefits, without any limitation as to the unlawfulness of their source. The legislator ignored the question of the location of this measure in the civil law system and provided it without any comment on its relationship with other civil measures (as for example recovery of unjust enrichment[15]). This problem was present in the Polish literature and judicature also before the implementation of the Enforcement Directive. The laconic regulation of this measure leads to the discrepancy in the interpretation of its content.

Namely, it is unclear whether this measure should be treated as a form of claim based on unjust enrichment or it is a special *sui generis* claim, typical for the protection of the intellectual property rights. The Polish legal doctrine and judicature are not unanimous in their opinion as to the nature and scope of this measure.[16] There are recent decisions of the Supreme Court which are contradictory.[17] The most controversial is the scope of this claim (all the profits made by infringer, only profits gained as a result of the exploitation of the intellectual property right or only the saved expenditures in form of royalty rates). In many statements the scope of this claim is conditioned by certain goals imposed on it. Namely, according to some commentators it has to have a deterrent and repres-

15 There is no reference to the general rules of civil law in present regulation (as it was previously in some regulations). In Polish law it is also impossible to use the institution of *negotiorum gestio* to explain the nature and scope of this claim, as it is often made in German judicature and doctrine.

16 Recently R. Skubisz, *Roszczenie o wydanie bezpodstawnie uzyskanych korzyści*, in: R. Skubisz, A. Kidyba (ed.), *Współczesne problemy prawa handlowego. Księga jubileuszowa dedykowana prof. dr hab. Marii Poźniak-Niedzielskiej*, p. 311 (Kraków 2007) - expressing the view that this is claim for recovery of unjust enrichment; M. du Vall in: E. Nowińska, U. Promińska, M. du Vall: *Prawo własności przemysłowej*, p. 154 (Warszawa 2008) - treating this claim as unconnected with the regime of unjust enrichment.

17 Cf. Polish Supreme Court of 24 October 2007, Case IV CSK 203/07, OSNC 2009, No. 1, para. 13, in which the Court declared that unlawfully obtained profits do not constitute unjust enrichment and the decision of the Supreme Court under previously binding regulation of 10 August 2006, Case V CSK 237/06 (unpublished), which refers in the interpretation of this claim to the regime of unjust enrichment.

sive effect on the infringer and, consequently, it should involve all the profits made by the infringer without any relationship to the loss incurred by the right holder. This sort of interpretation I find very dangerous.[18]

First of all, no clear regulation deepens the practical problems with use of this measure in Polish law. Therefore, in my opinion, it is necessary to clarify the nature of this measure, putting aside the goals and opinions presented for one's immediate needs. In Polish civil law there is no place to include the infringer's profits in the frames of compensation for damages sustained by the right holder. Only in certain situations, infringer's profits may constitute an indicator of the right holder loss, but this is an exceptional situation and should be justified by the proofs of the clear relationship between these two amounts.[19] Secondly, if this measure is treated as a *sui generis* claim, besides the claim for recovery of unjust enrichment which is always available[20] typical for the liability for the intellectual property rights infringements, then its nature should be clarified. Otherwise this measure may constitute a danger for the freedom to trade. It should be emphasized that this measure may be used in case of innocent infringements (see also Art. 13 (2) of the Enforcement Directive).[21] Consequently, the infringer who did not know or did not have reasonable grounds to know, engaged in the illegal activity is obliged to recover all profits he made. In my opinion such a *sui generis* measure should be used only in cases of culpable infringements.[22] In Polish civil law in case of material goods a comparable claim is applied only in case of possession in bad faith. According to the rules of Polish property law, good faith justifies the illegal fructification of other people's property. I find no grounds for such privileging protection of the intellectual property. Therefore, in the process of the harmonization of Polish law the optional provision of Art. 13 (2) of the Enforcement Directive should have been omitted. Meanwhile, it was included to Polish law in a hybrid form which generates numerous problems.

18 Cf. A. Kur, *Prävention - Cui Bono? Überlegungen zur Schadensersatzberechnung im Immaterialgüterrecht*, in: *"... und sie bewegt sich doch!" - Patent law on the move. Festschrift für G. Kolle und D. Stauder*, p. 375 (Cologne-Berlin-Bonn-Munich 2005).

19 See on this the controversial Polish Supreme Court of 11 October 2001, Case II CKN 578/99, OSN 2002, No. 6, para. 83; see for more A. Tischner, *Odpowiedzialność majątkowa z tytułu naruszenia prawa do znaku towarowego*, p. 93 (Warszawa 2008).

20 Different opinion presented R. Skubisz who states that the claim for recovery of profits is a form of claim for recovery of unjust enrichment. See *supra* note 16.

21 In the U.S. a comparable measure – account of profits - is accessible only in case of the intentional misconduct and constitutes a special sanction, conditioned on the character of the infringer's behaviour – deliberate, wilful, fraudulent. Compare Restatement (Third) of Unfair Competition (1995), § 37e.

22 Cf. A. Tischner (*supra* note 19), p. 215.

3. Injunctions and alternative measures

The claims for cease and desist and for removal of the infringement's effects (recall from the market and destruction) constitute the most important and effective measures of protection of the intellectual property rights by putting into practice the prevention aims. In the meantime, as a result of the harmonization the general claim for the removal of the infringement's effects has been withdrawn from the Industrial Property Law (Art. 287) and replaced by the strict claim for the removal from the market (Art. 286) which corresponds to Art. 10 of the Enforcement Directive. Consequently, a very useful measure has been substituted by a measure which is also important but limited in its scope to the described acts of the infringer. No other way of removing the results of the infringement which are not listed in Art. 286 of the Industrial Property Law is accessible. This way of improving the enforcement of the intellectual property deserves criticisms. Moreover, pursuant to the optional Art. 12 of the Directive the alternative measure was included in Polish law. Namely in Art. 287 (3) of the Industrial Property Law and in Art. 79 (3) of the Copyright Act it is stated that, if the act of infringement was committed unintentionally, the court may order that infringer to pay the right holder an adequate amount of money if the cessation of the infringement or the decision on recall from the market would be excessively severe for the infringer person and the payment of the adequate sum of money properly meets the interests of the right holder. Although this measure may have some practical relevance, its nature is unclear and unknown for the system of Polish law.

4. Right to information

The only and real gain for Polish law from the implementing the Directive is the right to information which was nearly absent in the Polish intellectual property law. The obligatory Art. 8 of the Enforcement Directive forced the Polish legislator to provide this measure. Before the amendment the rudimentary regulation of this measure was present in the Copyright Act.[23] The legal doctrine emphasized the need of such a measure for the effective enforcement of other claims,[24]

23 Cf. former version of Art. 80 of the Copyright Act.

24 Among others: P. Magnuski, A. Tomaszek, *O potrzebie roszczenia o informację w prawach dotyczących ochrony własności przemysłowej i czynów nieuczciwej konkurencji*, 2001 Monitor Prawniczy, 967; A. Kołodziej, *Roszczenie informacyjne w prawie własności intelektualnej*, in: *Księga Pamiątkowa ku czci prof. J. Szwaji*, 88 ZNUJ PWiOWI 145 (2004).

taking into account quite strict rules of assessment of damages in Polish civil law. The nature of the intellectual property infringements results in information asymmetry which may be removed with the right to information. However, one should take into account the extraordinary nature of this measure.

The main problem met in the implementation of the right to information was the nature of this measure: the procedural or substantive claim and its relationship to other measures of gathering and preserving the evidence and rules of civil procedure. The right to information provided in the Copyright Act (Art. 80) is drafted very broadly. Namely, the right holder may request from the infringer any information which is essential for other claims. No limitation as to its scope is included. Moreover, such motion may be filed with the court also prior to filing a suit. Meanwhile, according to Art. 8 of the Directive, the information may be requested in the context of proceedings concerning an infringement of an intellectual property right and in response to a justified and proportionate request of the claimant. The infringer's obligation to provide the information is not limited to the acts carried on a commercial scale. Such a broad obligation may be the object of malpractice and use for purposes other than laying claims. The scope of obligation to provide information of persons other than the infringer is drafted in accordance with the requirements of Art. 8 of the Enforcement Directive. It is limited to the acts carried on a commercial scale. The very open regulation of the right to information in the Copyright Act causes that in practice the courts should control its use taking into account proportionality and justification of this measure in particular cases. Moreover, courts have to put this measure in the procedural frames because in the regulation of the right to information we find no suggestion as to this aspect.

The right to information in case of an infringement of industrial property rights is regulated in Art. 286^1 of the Industrial Property Law which provides for that the application for the information necessary in enforcing the claims may be filed with the court even before an action is brought, where the likelihood of infringement of these rights is high. This limitation constitutes a certain step forward in comparison with the regulation of this measure in the Copyright Act. The right to information may be requested from persons other than the infringer only in the case of activities that are intended to directly or indirectly gain profit or other economic benefits (the activities of customers in good faith being excluded there from). However, the procedural form imposed for enforcing this measure (i.e. the provisional procedure to preserve the claims) is astonishing.

To sum up, let's hope that courts will use this measure reasonably since a very open and incomplete regulation may be misused to explore the data of competitors. In the Polish regulation of the right to information there are no provisions protecting the interests of a person giving information. There is also no regulation relating to the use of the obtained information in other disputes. Again we can observe that the regulation which was to improve the enforcement of the intellectual property caused numerous doubts and may be the source of abuse.

IV. Conclusions

First of all, we should ask whether we have strong grounds to treat certain areas of private (civil) law in such a special, privileged way. Undoubtedly, immaterial nature of the intellectual property constitutes a justification for such a special treatment. Particular circumstances and forms of infringements (esp. piracy and counterfeiting) may constitute a temptation to use the stricter measures to combat such phenomena. A legal system, in which protection of certain goods is created, may not tolerate their infringement without sanction. However, the protection of certain goods does not constitute the absolute value which justifies the manipulation of legal measures. We should remember that the main goal of the Enforcement Directive is to be achieved by application of its specific measures to all infringements including those which are not wilful and fraudulent and those which are not carried out on commercial scale.

In my opinion the civil liability for intellectual property law infringement should be drafted in a balanced way. This remark refers especially to the common belief that the scope of the maximum prevention gives good results in the enforcement of intellectual property rights. Obviously, underdeterrence reduces the incentives to act in line with the law. However, overdeterrence has a chilling effect.[25] In the commercial activity certain risk is unavoidable. The decision on the shape of civil liability in the intellectual property law requires consideration of such an effect. The rules of liability which disregard bases of liability, especially the requirement of fault, may have a very negative influence on the legal system and on level of commercial activity of the citizens as intellectual property rights are indicating the border between exclusivity and freedom.

Therefore a specific regulation of liability for intellectual property infringements should be faced with the classic civil law rules. It is very important to draft regulations of the liability for infringements of intellectual property rights in a way which will result in balanced effects, especially as regards the prevention effect. Underdeterrence in this area reduces incentives to act legally. On the contrary, overdeterrence, which manifests itself in reducing any activity connected with a risk of liability and uncertainty as to its legality.[26] The modification

25 This problem is discussed by A. Kur (*supra* note 2), p. 829.

26 This situation is described in the American literature by P. Heald, *Money Damages and Corrective Advertising. An Economic Analysis*, 55 University of Chicago Law Review 647 (1988).

of behaviour goes beyond the legal requirements. It reduces the scope of and costs of production and marketing which influences negatively the market and the competition as the costs of diligent behaviour are very high (e.g. costs of legal opinions). Consequently, the general prevention in order to protect certain goods (i.e. intellectual property goods) acts as a break on any economic activity.

The preventive effect of certain regulations may result from the principle of responsibility. The full preventive influence may be observed in case of liability based on the principle of fault, as it may impact on the level of diligence. The motivating influence of liability regulations may be observed in cases when it possible to avoid damage acting diligently. The measure which provides for the payment of damages (esp. double) or the recovery of all profits in cases of innocent infringements have no preventive influence. In such cases prevention against the infringements of intellectual property becomes prevention against any kind of activity which refers to intellectual property.

Therefore, it is necessary to retain the balance between the protection of interests of individual groups. Civil liability for the intellectual property law infringements combines the tension between the necessity of sufficient protection of the exclusivity and the provision of freedom to trade.[27] When drafting the rules of this liability one should avoid to attribute the responsibility for the infringement to a person, only because it was uncertain to estimate the risk of certain activity. The rules of liability, based only on the principle of deterrence, which violate the classic rules of civil law, especially those which eliminate the prerequisite of fault, may result in a very negative influence on the legal system and economic development.

In my opinion implementation, as a process of including certain rules in the existing national system, should not consist in the break of the foundations of this system. The specificity of the Polish situation as regards intellectual property protection, especially economic backwardness resulting from the political factors after the Second World War and the relatively low social consciousness in this area, resulted in a certain shift of focus. Namely, it is generally believed that a severe sanction constitutes the most efficient measure aimed at combating the intellectual property infringements. Unfortunately, the Enforcement Directive has strongly encouraged this way of thinking about liability for the intellectual property infringements.

Instead of providing the coherence in the system of private law, the implementation of the Enforcement Directive into the Polish law lead to the fragmentation and disorder, especially by providing measures which are alien to the civil law, e.g. a special regulation of payment of damages or recovery of profits. I am

27 Cf. Ch. Geiger, *"Constitutionalising" Intellectual Property Law? The Influence of Fundamental Rights on Intellectual Property in the European Union*, 37 IIC 371 (2006).

afraid that nobody examined in details the need and the results of such special regulations disregarding classical civil law rules. Under the banner of the efficient protection of the intellectual property, the hybrids are formed which are not reflected in the existing legal systems (e.g. the German as well as Polish judicial practice of including the infringer's profit within the frames of damages). The regulation of civil liability constitutes the system rich in measures, which are suitably nuanced. "The landscape" after the infringement of the intellectual property forces to look for different measures. The attempt at making one measure (e.g. payment of damages) the only remedy for the complex effects of the infringements leads to its degeneration. Meanwhile, it is necessary to examine the functions and the prerequisites of each measure, taking into account the specifics of the intellectual property (e.g. payment of damages, recovery of unjust enrichment, etc.).

Interlocutory Injunctions in IP Disputes under Polish Law

Tomasz Targosz

Introduction

Preliminary injunctions are of utmost importance in intellectual property disputes. Usually, the plaintiff wants the on-going infringement to be stopped, and since the proceedings may eventually drag for years, a preliminary injunction remains the only way to effectively achieve this aim.[1] However, since preliminary injunctions, by their very nature, require certain concessions in favour of the plaintiff, there always lingers the problem of adequate protection of the interests of the defendant. Legal rules must strike a compromise between effective enforcement and the general principle of the legal system, according to which deciding disputes between private individuals may be done only in court proceedings, in which both parties have the right to be heard before the decision is given. In the context of IP rights infringements several additional factors must be taken into account when discussing preliminary injunctions in the Polish procedural law. Firstly, certain requirements concerning preliminary injunctions stem from the European law, i.e. the Directive 2004/48/EC of the European Parliament and of the Council of 29 April 2004 on the enforcement of intellectual property rights.[2] It is important not only because of the obvious obligation to correctly implement the provisions of the directive. Since Community law has so far affected procedural rules of EU Members States to a limited extent,[3] and it is unlikely to harmonise national procedures in the foreseeable future, the conspicuous difficulty here is how to preserve the coherence and inner logic of national procedural systems.[4] IP disputes are important, but it would be rather

1 A. Jakubecki, R. Skubisz, *Zabezpieczenie roszczeń wynikających z naruszenia prawa z rejestracji znaku towarowego,* 50 ZNUJ 103 (1989).

2 Corrigendum to Directive 2004/48/EC of the European Parliament and of the Council of 29 April 2004 on the enforcement of intellectual property rights, OJ EU L 157 of 30 April 2004, p. 45.

3 Of course there may be some exceptions, but it would be difficult to argue that national civil procedures have been harmonized to any extent. See M. Tulibacka, *Europeanization of Civil Procedures: In Search of a Coherent Approach,* (2009) 5 CMLR 1527.

4 The Directive explicitly states in its recital 11 that it *"does not aim to establish harmonised rules for judicial cooperation, jurisdiction, the recognition and enforcement of decisions in civil and commercial matters, or deal with applicable law. There are Commu-*

strange if preliminary injunctions in these cases, while serving basically the same functions as injunctions in other types of disputes, differed in the most fundamental ways from the "general" injunctions. It is not only the question of elegance – practically a system of injunctions in IP disputes must be to a greater or lesser extent embedded in the general system of injunctions in a given procedural law. Therefore, these general provisions of procedural law will apply also to injunctions in IP matters, and if they are incompatible, the effectiveness of injunctions in IP matters may suffer. Consequently, I am of the view that the principle of effectiveness of Community law requires in this particular case to shape the national legislation implementing the Enforcement Directive as closely as possible to the existing national regime,[5] while of course providing for all the guarantees and instruments the Directive requires.[6] This should not be an impossible task, as I believe, much of what the Directive seeks to introduce is not entirely new to at least most of the Members States.

Secondly, the question arises, to what extent IP matters should be treated differently than other types of cases. To avoid any misunderstandings, I must explain that the "system" of preliminary injunctions one may deduce from the Enforcement Directive could theoretically apply in all types of civil cases. As we will see, this is what the Polish legislator has in fact relied on, deciding not to introduce any new provisions on injunctions for industrial property rights disputes. The question is therefore whether there really exist compelling grounds (on a national level) to starkly differentiate the legal regime of preliminary injunctions in IP disputes from the general regime of preliminary injunctions. One should be careful not to overlook that this question is about law and not about facts. For example, preliminary injunctions usually require that the applicant makes his claim credible by showing that he is the right holder and that there has been a breach of his right by the defendant (the required standard of evidence may be lower than during the 'proper' trial). With registered rights it is manifestly easy to comply with this requirement, at least as regards proving the plaintiff is the right holder, but this does not mean that the legal rule making granting

nity instruments which govern such matters in general terms and are, in principle, equally applicable to intellectual property.".

5 As some claim that the procedural harmonization undertaken by the Directive may have been premature (G. Cumming, M. Freudenthal, R. Janal, *Enforcement of Intellectual Property Rights in Dutch, English and German Civil Courts* (2008)) one may argue that only a cautious implementation is reasonable. Since harmonization has not been achieved, a Member State that would attempt to follow closely community concepts would end up jeopardizing the consistency of its national law without reaching the aim of community harmonisation.

6 The Directive does not provide for any definition of a preliminary injunction - Ch. Heinze, *Einstweiliger Rechtsschutz im europäischen Immaterialgüterrecht,* p. 79 et seq. (Tübingen 2007).

an injunction conditional on furnishing proof of the violated right should be any different. It will be easier to meet in IP cases, but that's all.

There are several issues about preliminary injunctions that merit special attention, and I believe define the very nature of this procedural instrument. They in fact reflect the consecutive stages of the procedure, perceived from the perspective of the applicant (but since there are two parties to the proceedings they are relevant for the defendant accordingly). At the first stage, the question is what types of claims may be brought before court and secured by means of a preliminary injunction, what the applicant has to show (conditions) and what types of injunctions may be issued. Two other important aspects are the role of the defendant (whether the opponent must be heard before the injunction is granted) and what remedies are available for both parties and especially for the defendant.

The second stage is the stage of enforcement, i.e. how injunctions are enforced and whether enforcement is sufficiently effective.

The third stage is only pertinent if it turns out that the injunction should not have been granted. The question arises whether the plaintiff and applicant should pay damages to the defendant and on what grounds.

Before venturing any further I must introduce one restriction of the subject-matter of the ensuing presentation, and it so happens, that the reason for this limitation touches upon the nature of preliminary injunctions. The question which has not been yet asked above is: what is a preliminary injunction? The Enforcement Directive regulates measures for obtaining or preserving evidence (Art. 6 and 7), right of information (Art. 8) and finally provisional and precautionary measures (Art. 9). It has been argued that what differentiates preliminary injunctions as a separate legal concept is that this instrument is available before the dispute is finally decided and is not tantamount to a final decision on the merits of the case. Under this view measures concerning evidence and possibly also information claims could be regarded as falling under the concept of a preliminary injunction.[7] This is of course a matter of perspective but I will not follow it for the purpose of this short outline of Polish law because of the assumption I have already made above. Although it may be justified to talk of an "abstract" model of a preliminary injunction from the perspective of comparative law or a concept of preliminary injunction in Community law[8] (both before

7 E.g. Ch. Heinze (*supra* note 6), p. 102 et seq.

8 However in the judgment of 28 April 2005, Case C-115/03 - *St. Paul Dairy Industries NV*, the ECJ stated that a "*measure ordering the hearing of a witness for the purpose of enabling the applicant to decide whether to bring a case, determine whether it would be well founded and assess the relevance of evidence which might be adduced in that regard is not covered by the notion of 'provisional, including protective, measures'.*" As this would be a rather clear example of a measure concerning evidence, it is apparent that Community law does not require such measures to be treated as provisional measures in

Community courts and in the meaning of Community procedural regulations), there still exist national concepts of preliminary injunctions. The Enforcement Directive does not intend to alter them in any way and since such alterations at the present stage of harmonization of procedural laws (or lack of it) would lead to undesirable results, they should be avoided. Under Polish law preliminary injunctions should be conceptually separated from measures concerning evidence and information rights. I also find this result absolutely correct, as it is not only a question of systematization and legal definitions. The differences are of fundamental nature and should affect legal rules applying to each of these instruments. A preliminary injunction in the strict sense is a correlate of a substantive or procedural claim.[9] Its purpose is to ensure that the goal of the civil proceedings from the point of view of the plaintiff[10] could be reached and its underlying assumption is that for this to happen it is sometimes required to take some provisional measures before the final decision on the merits is delivered. It is here that the tension between the need to protect the interests of the right holder and the principle according to which obligations may be imposed on private persons only by final court *judgements* issued in proceedings in which each party has the right to be heard is the most conspicuous. Measures concerning evidence have the purpose of helping the plaintiff to prove his claim and this is also generally true of the so called information rights. Here the tension (conflict of interests) is of a more procedural nature and affects especially the right not to be forced to incriminate oneself. The Polish civil procedure clearly differentiates between preliminary injunctions and evidence issues. Consequently I will only refer to the first category. I will also try to focus my attention on these types of preliminary injunctions that seem characteristic of IP disputes, i.e. forbidding or preventing infringements and seizures of infringing goods. By contrast, seizure of property, the purpose of which is to ensure that the plaintiff may recover damages,[11] is not in any sense typical of IP disputes. The factors determining whether to apply this measure should solely concentrate on issues pertinent to the defendant, and the fact that the dispute in question concerns IP rights is of no relevance.

the strict sense of this term. Also in its decision on Case C-261/90, ECR *1992, I-02149 - Reichert, the ECJ found that "Provisional or protective measures within the meaning of Article 24 must be understood as being measures which, in matters within the scope of the Convention, are intended to preserve a factual or legal situation so as to safeguard rights the recognition of which is sought elsewhere from the court having jurisdiction as to the substance of the matter." This is again close to the view I share in this paper.*

9 The latter view is the prevailing one – D. Zawistowski, *Postępowanie zabezpieczające. Komentarz. Wybór orzeczeń,* p. 30 (Warszawa 2007).

10 In other words, one could say that preliminary injunctions safeguard legally protected interests of the plaintiff/right holder.

11 Art. 9 (2) of the Enforcement Directive.

Preliminary injunctions in Polish Law – The General Picture

A brief analysis of the Polish law relevant for preliminary injunctions should help us to establish to what extent the law had to be amended when implementing the enforcement Directive, and whether the current state of affairs can be perceived as an example of over-protection, under-protection or maybe adequate protection of IP rights.

Under Polish law on Civil Procedure preliminary injunctions may secure all types of claims.[12] Limitations may however stem from some principles of injunctions procedure, the most important of which has been codified in Art. 731 CCP. It says that securing a claim may not be tantamount to satisfying it,[13] unless the law expressly provides otherwise.[14] Injunctions may be granted during trial or before a trial is initiated.[15] Generally, the applicant must satisfy two conditions: credibility of the claim and 'legal interest'. Credibility of the claim implies some preliminary legal assessment, however the standard of evidence is lower than it would be in the "regular" proceedings. However, although courts tend to emphasise this every time giving grounds for injunction decisions, one must be aware that in practice it all very much depends on the circumstances of the case, for e.g. the type of the alleged infringement. With regard to proving that the applicant is the right holder credibility may be in fact equal to definitive proof (e.g. registration certificate). If the circumstances of the case are such that the facts are mostly undisputable and the real controversies are on the points of law, there may be no discernible difference between the required standard of proof. "Legal interest" is defined is Art. 730^1 CCP as a situation in which a refusal to grant the injunction could make impossible or seriously impair enforcement of the final decision or could make impossible or seriously impair achieving the goal of the proceedings. Legal interest therefore contains the requirement of urgency.[16] The applicant must show, to put it in layman's terms, why it is not sufficient to wait for the final outcome of the proceedings, that is why protection must be granted immediately. However, the concept of legal interest has been deliberately designed to be a little broader[17] so that it could accommodate other relevant factors. It allows for example to deny an injunction to the plaintiff, who has failed to react in due time

12 Art. 730 § 1 CCP specifically provides that injunctions may be granted in all types of civil matters.

13 Polish Supreme Court of 11 May 1983, Case II CZ 51/83, LexPolonica No. 321051; of 17 February 1986, Case IV CZ 17/86, LexPolonica No. 320989.

14 Such examples are provided in Art. 753 and 7531 CCP (e.g. paying of alimony).

15 Art. 730 § 2 CCP.

16 The requirement of urgency can be also described as universally accepted, including Community law – M. Pechstein, *EU-/EG-Prozessrecht,* p. 481 f. (Tübingen 2007).

17 D. Zawistowski (*supra* note 9), p. 30-31.

to the infringement and has filed a claim after a considerable amount of time has passed.

The balance[18] of interests constitutes another underlying principle of the CCP provisions in injunction proceedings. Art. 730^1 § 3 CCP states that when selecting the method of securing the claim the court will take account of the interests of both parties and will choose a method giving adequate protection while avoiding putting unnecessary burdens on the defendant.

The playing field for the court, as regards the shape of the injunction, is rather broad. The court may apply usual measures such as seizure of property or freezing of bank accounts, may forbid the defendant to dispose of his property or may order the defendant to act in a certain manner (e.g. continue to perform under a contract) or restrain from certain actions.

Motions for preliminary injunctions should be decided within a week, but there are no consequences if this time limit is not observed. In fact, it very rarely is.

Decisions on preliminary injunctions are usually issued without hearing the defendant in the first instance.[19] although procedural rules allow to hold a hearing.[20] This possibility is almost never used. Therefore the court of the first instance may base its decision only on the motion for a preliminary injunction and the evidence attached to it. The defendant learns about the injunction either by receiving a copy from the court or from the court's executioner, should the injunction require execution (e.g. seizure of goods or other property). The injunction may be appealed[21] within 7 days after the defendant has received it and this is most commonly at this stage, when he is able for the first time to present his position on the matter.[22] The decision of the appellate court is final in that there

18 It is also recognized in Community law: Order of the President of the Court of 19 July 1995, Case C-149/95, para. 55 - *Atlantic Container Line AB*.

19 This enables to issue the injunction more quickly and makes it harder for the defendant to pre-empt the injunction, thus frustrating its enforcement. On the other hand often injunctions have very serious consequences and a hearing could help to better balance the interests of the parties. See J. Fiołka, *Wniosek o zabezpieczenie roszczenia o zaniechanie naruszenia w prawie ochrony własności intelektualnej*, 69 ZNUJ 27, 30 (1997). In my opinion if there is no risk that a hearing could thwart effective enforcement courts should be more willing to let the defendant have his say.

20 T. Erecinski in: M. Jędrzejewska, T. Ereciński, J. Gudowski, *Kodeks postępowania cywilnego. Komentarz. Część pierwsza. Postępowanie rozpoznawcze. Część druga, Postępowanie zabezpieczające*, Art. 735, No. 1 (Warszawa 2007); J. Jagieła in: K. Piasecki, *Kodeks postępowania cywilnego*, Vol. II, p. 462 (Warszawa 2006).

21 Art. 741 CCP.

22 Arguments put forward by the defendant may of course attack the credibility of the claim and the appellate court must consider them since credibility of the claim should be assed also in the light of *contra* arguments: Polish Supreme Court of 9 September 1961, Case IV CZ 54/61, OSNC 1963, No. 6, para. 114.

is no cassation to the Supreme Court,[23] however the injunction may expire because of other reasons, e.g. when the claim is dismissed in the proceedings on the merits. If the circumstances change,[24] the defendant may move to repeal or modify the injunction.[25] (e.g. if the IP right such as a patent is declared invalid by the Patent Office the court will repeal the injunction granted on its basis even if it had been appealed against unsuccessfully[26]). However, if the factual circumstances do not change, the final injunction may not be changed or repealed until the end of the proceedings on the merits.[27]

The applicant, when successful in obtaining the injunction, must initiate proceedings on the merits within the deadline stipulated by the court in the injunction itself. The deadline may not exceed 14 days. In practice the courts almost never apply shorter time limits, therefore the maximum time limit provided for in Art. 733 CCP is standard. If the proceedings are not initiated, the injunction expires.

Enforcement of an injunction depends to a large extent on its content. Injunctions ordering the defendant to cease infringing actions are so to say enforceable by themselves. If the defendant does not comply, the plaintiff may demand that penalty payments be imposed on the defendant.[28] However, the amount of the fine may not exceed 1000 PLN and only after three fines within these limits have proven unsuccessful the court may order the defendant to pay a higher sum, but not more than 100.000 PLN in total. Only if penalty fines have not been paid, the court may "convert" them into arrest.[29] If the defendant is a legal person, the fine is imposed on the natural person (employee) responsible for failure to comply with the injunction,[30] or, when it proves difficult to establish who that was, on the person authorised to represent the legal person (e.g. the managing board member). It is not difficult to notice that this mechanism can hardly be described as effective. Of course non-compliance is illegal and justifies damages, but the

23 This being one of the reasons why the decisions of the judiciary are rarely published.

24 Polish Supreme Court of 23 August 1989, Case II CZ 135/89 (unpublished).

25 Art. 742 § 1 CCP.

26 A. Jakubecki, *Postępowanie zabezpieczające w sprawach z zakresu prawa własności intelektualnej,* p. 403 (Kraków 2002); Z. Hahn, *Środki prawne w postępowaniu zabezpieczającym,* PPC 13-18/1938, p. 980; Wrocław District Court of 27 July 2009, Case X GC 115/09 (unpublished); Wrocław Court of Appeal of 30 October 2009, Case I ACz 1374/09 (unpublished).

27 See A. Jakubecki (*supra* note 26), p. 402. It is controversial whether the dismissal of the claim in the first instance may be regarded as a change in the circumstances of the case, allowing to repeal or modify the injunction under Art. 742 CCP.

28 R. Tomczyk, *Zagadnienia proceduralne w sprawach o naruszenie praw własności przemysłowej ze szczególnym uwzględnieniem zabezpieczenia i egzekucji,* 80 ZNUJ PWIOWI 268 (2002).

29 Art. 1051-1053 CCP.

30 Art. 1053 § 2 CCP.

injunction in such a case does not give anything extra, as illegality follows from the infringement itself.

Finally, at the last stage, i.e. if the plaintiff fails to win the case and the injunction expires or is repealed for a number of reasons, the Polish law allows the defendant to pursue damages against the applicant. The crucial provision here is Art. 746 CCP. Unlike the majority of CCP provisions on provisional injunctions, which one may agree with or not, but which have been drafted in an acceptable manner, Art. 746 CCP is a particularly inept contrivance that has to be interpreted *contra legem* in order to preserve the most basic sense of fairness and common sense. To begin with, injunctions expire if the statement of claim is not filed (usually) within 14 days, the statement of claim or motion is withdrawn, rejected or dismissed, the proceedings are discontinued or the judgment becomes final (however, when the Supreme Court quashes the judgment there is no 'resurrection' of the injunction). Damages can be claimed only when the injunction expires for a reason given in Art. 746 CCP. This provision reads as follows:

> § 1. If the applicant has not filed the submission initiating the proceedings in the specified time period or has withdrawn the claim or the motion or if the claim has been returned or rejected or the claim or motion have been dismissed as unfounded or when the proceedings have been discontinued as well as in cases specified in Art. 744 § 2 CCP,[31] the defendant may demand compensation for the damages caused by the enforcement of the injunction. This claim expires if it has not been pursued within a year since the damage occurred.
>
> § 2. The applicants who have obtained the injunction jointly shall be jointly liable for damages referred to in § 1.
>
> § 3. Should the defendant fail to file a claim within a month from the day the claim referred to in § 1 arose, the court shall return to the applicant, at his motion, the pledge deposited to secure this claim.

The most conspicuous problem one should immediately notice is the time bar. The concept of damage in Polish civil law understands damage as independent of unlawfulness and fault, i.e. being just one of the conditions of liability. Should the said provision be interpreted literally, claims for damages could not be pursued, because the claim would expire before it could be filed in court[32] - damage usually starts to accrue immediately after the injunction has been enforced and it is highly uncommon for civil proceedings to end in one year. What makes matters worse is that Art. 746 before amendment read: „the claim expires if the debtor has not pursued it within a year after it arose", which did not cause any

31 I.e. when the applicant did not file a statement of the claim covering the entire claim he demanded injunction for or when the statement of the claim covers a different claim than the one injunction was sought for.

32 S. Sołtysiński, A. Nowicka, *Uwagi o projekcie ustawy wdrażającej Dyrektywę 2004/48/WE w sprawie egzekwowania praw własności intelektualnej,* 4 KPP 1078 (2006).

problems in this respect.[33] It seems however, that courts tend to disregard the literal wording of Art. 746 CCP and assume that the time limit for filing the claim for damages starts to run on the day, the judgment on the merits[34] has become final.[35]

According to the prevailing view liability for damages caused by the injunction is strict,[36] i.e. not based on the requirement of fault on the part of the applicant.[37] This is however not a unanimous opinion. Proponents of the fault based liability[38] point out to the fact that there are other claims known in the Polish procedural law, resulting from incorrect court decisions and they are generally based on fault, that if the injunction is issued in arbitration proceedings the applicant will be liable only if the injunction was manifestly incorrect (Art. 1182 CCP), which, it is suggested, implies fault, and finally that in Polish tort law liability is as a rule based on fault, therefore if one wants to depart from this principle this should be clearly signalled. Apart from that one should consider that even Art. 746 CCP itself does not introduce strict liability – such a view requires recourse to the provisions of the Civil Code on strict liability, especially to rule out liability where the damage is solely caused by the defendant, a third party or a result of *force majeure*.

It is also assumed that the part of the provision reading *caused by the enforcement of the injunction* should be interpreted as meaning "caused by the injunction". This is because injunctions may be divided into enforceable and non-enforceable injunctions. For example bans to market the product usually do not require any additional action on the part of the issuing court (or the court's exe-

33 The preparatory works do not explain the reason for the amendment.

34 Or the decision sanctioning discontinuance of the proceedings or rejection of the claim for formal reasons.

35 A. Kubas, *Odpowiedzialność za szkodę wyrządzoną wykonaniem zabezpieczenia (Art. 746, 1182 k.p.c.),* 3-4 TPP 71 (2006); Gdańsk Court of Appeal of 20 June 2008, Case I ACa 533/08 (unpublished); Kraków Court of Appeal of 8 December 2009, Case IACa 906/2009 (unpublished).

36 E. Wengerek, *Postępowanie zabezpieczające i egzekucyjne,* p. 50 f. (Warszawa 1972); W. Siedlecki in: Z. Resich, W. Siedlecki (ed.), *Kodeks postępowania cywilnego. Komentarz, cz. II, Postępowanie zabezpieczające i egzekucyjne,* p. 1066 (Warszawa 1976); A. Zieliński in: A. Zieliński, *Kodeks postępowania cywilnego, t. II, Komentarz do artykułów 506 - 1217,* p. 502 (Warszawa 2006); M. Irzykowski, *Naprawienie szkody wyrządzonej zabezpieczeniem,* Palestra 10/1979, 3 f.; A. Karnicka-Kawczyńska, J. Kawczyński, *Postępowanie zabezpieczające w praktyce sądowej,* 1999 Monitor Prawniczy No. 4, 25; Poznań Court of Appeal of 8 February 2007, Case I ACa 1138/06 (unpublished). More nuanced approach but also acknowledging objective liability: Kraków Court of Appeal of 8 December 2009, Case IACa 906/2009 (unpublished).

37 However, liability is excluded by force majeure, sole fault of the injured party or of a third party the defendant is not liable for – M. Irzykowski (*supra* note 36), p. 3.

38 A. Kubas (*supra* note 35), p. 62 et seq.

cutioner), if the defendant complies of his own will. Read literally, liability would be excluded with regard to this type of injunctions, which certainly does not make much sense.[39]

If we look at the above sketched picture with the Enforcement Directive in mind, we may conclude the Polish law did not require many amendments. It would go beyond the scope of this short paper to elucidate each and every detail of the Enforcement Directive and in particular its Art. 9, but let us briefly summarise the fundamental obligations the Directive imposes on EU Member States. General provisions of the Polish CCP ensure that the right-holder may apply for an interlocutory injunction, also before proceedings on the merits are initiated, and the injunction may prevent an imminent infringement or forbid a continuing one.[40] Seizure of infringing goods may be ordered as well.[41] Injunctions subject to a recurring penalty payment are not provided under Polish law, hence there was no obligation to introduce them in IP matters. With regard to Art. 9 (1) of the Directive, the only solution that does not exist under Polish law is a possibility to file for an injunction against a service-provider, who himself does not have to be an infringer. Seizure of property (Art. 9 (2) of the Directive) or blocking of bank accounts are also guaranteed and not restricted to commercial matters, but this should be admissible as the Directive strives for a minimum harmonization only. The requirements of credibility of the claim and legal interest do justice to the provision of Art. 9 (3) of the Directive. With regard to the possibility of taking provisional measures without hearing the defendant the Polish law again goes farther than the Directive demands. In my opinion this could be only questioned by referring to the concept of fundamental rights, possibly also the ECHR, but most likely, the solution adopted in CCP should be considered acceptable also from this point of view. Appeal is granted and so is the obligation to institute proceedings on the merits of the case (Art. 9 (5) of the Enforcement Directive). What may be controversial, however, is the fact that the Polish law does not require any request of the defendant for the expiry of the injunction to take place if proceedings on the merits are not initiated. However, although the consequence is automatic (*ex lege*),[42] Art. 744 § 3 in conjunction with Art. 754^1 § 3 CCP allow the defendant to request that the court issue a decision confirming the expiry of the injunction. This should be sufficient to guarantee compatibility with the Directive. As already mentioned, damages are available for injuries

39 A. Kubas (*supra* note 35), p. 58; A. Jakubecki (in) *Kodeks postępowania cywilnego. Praktyczny komentarz*, Art. 746, No. 1 (Kraków 2005); Kraków Court of Appeal of 8 December 2009, Case I ACa 906/2009 (unpublished).

40 A. Jakubecki (*supra* note 26), p. 320 et seq.

41 A. Jakubecki (*supra* note 26), p. 325 et seq.

42 J. Jagieła (*supra* note 20), p. 459.

caused by provisional measures (Art. 9 (7)),[43] and the Directive constitutes one more reason to depart from the literal meaning of Art. 746 CCP (the Polish courts have chosen this path on their own, anyway). Finally, Art. 739 § 1 CCP allows to make the provisional injunction conditional on the lodging of security (Art. 9 (6)). As I have already stated, Member States should enjoy considerable leeway with regard to procedural details of implementing the rights and instruments covered by the Enforcement Directive. One should consequently avoid giving a detailed autonomous interpretation to these instruments. Rather, one should understand the Directive as forming basic obligations, i.e. requiring Members States to ensure that national legislation remains in essence in line with the solutions and instruments the Directive wants Member States to make available to right holders and defendants in IP disputes.

Special provisions in IP statutes

The Polish legislator decided to implement the Enforcement Directive[44] making amendments in statutes concerning various intellectual property rights. Only one provision of the CCP has been changed as a consequence of implementing the Directive,[45] although a large part of the Directive has been devoted to procedural instruments. Instead procedural matters have been introduced into IP statutes, which was not an entirely new concept in the field of copyright law, but a novelty for all the remaining IP legislation, including the Law on Industrial Property[46]. However, as far as interlocutory injunctions are concerned, special provisions have been only introduced into the Copyright Act[47] and their clone into the Act on Protection of Databases[48]. No provisions have been enacted with regard to industrial property rights, i.e. inter alia patents, designs and trademarks. Special provisions inserted into IP laws require further recourse to CCP, since they do not provide for a complete regulation. In other words, what has been done, are piecemeal adjustments only. The general concepts of CCP rules on injunctions

43 Strict liability should be regarded as admissible or possibly even preferred by the Directive.

44 Law of 9 May 2007, 99 Journal of Laws 662 (2007).

45 The amendment did not introduce any real changes but only corrected the wording of Art. 7531 CCP.

46 Law of 30 June 2000, consolidated text in 119 Journal of Laws 1117 (2003) with further amendments.

47 Law on Copyright and Neighbouring Rights of 4 February 1994, consolidated text in 90 Journal of Laws 631 (2006) with further amendments.

48 Law on the Protection of Databases of 27 July 2001, 128 Journal of Laws 1402 (2001) with further amendments.

have been left intact and the provisions of CCP must be applied almost in their entirety.

New provisions in Copyright law may be responsible for some confusion. The first change consists in wider jurisdiction of the injunction court. A motion for a preliminary injunction may be now filed with a court where the defendant carries out business activities or where his assets are located. This is not very precise and it is not explicitly required that the activity/assets in question should be somehow associated with the claim. In consequence, if the defendant carries out business activities all over Poland (which will be the rule as far as large enterprises are concerned) the motion may be practically filed everywhere. One can question the desirability of this solution, as it allows for forum shopping, and its practical significance should not be too easily downplayed. The main reason for this is the factor of time. Courts in Poland act usually much more quickly in smaller cities, than in Warsaw, Cracow or other bigger ones. Although, the court should decide the motion within a short time limit (more about it below), it is much more probable that the deadline will be met in smaller cities or towns. Thus the possibility to select the injunction court may be beneficial for the right holder. The second change is a modest one – the time limit for the court to take a decision whether to grant an interlocutory injunction in copyright cases is 3 days instead of 7 in 'normal' proceedings. Practically, both are hard to achieve. Additionally, the time limit for the appellate court has been set at 7 days, ever harder to meet in practice than the deadline for first instance courts.

The real question, however, is about the prerequisites of granting an injunction. Literal reading of Art. 80 of the Copyright Act could suggest the applicant must only show legal interest and no mention is made of the credibility of the claim. However, it is unacceptable to assume that the claim does not have to be credible,[49] as the results would be absurd and at the same time incompatible with the Enforcement Directive (legal interest, as explained above, does not require any showing that the claim has good prospects of being successful – this concept operates on a different level).

Another obvious mistake is an appearance of the obligatory 'bundling' of the motion for an injunction with a motion to secure evidence. Again literal interpretation must be discarded in order to reach a reasonable outcome.[50] It is hard to imagine why the applicant should have to file a motion to secure evidence *and* a

49 See P. Bogdalski, *Środki ochrony autorskich praw majątkowych oraz ich dochodzenie w świetle prawa polskiego,* p. 176 (Kraków 2003); Szczecin Court of Appeal of 6 January 2006, Case I ACz 1162/05, LexPolonica No. 279957*;* Lublin Court of Appeal of 12 February 1997, Case I ACz 38/97, Apel.-Lub. 1997/3/14; Warszawa Court of Appeal of 12 September 1995, Case I ACz 783/05 (unpublished).

50 J. Barta, R. Markiewicz, *Prawo autorskie,* p. 193 (Warszawa 2008).

motion to secure the claim (motion for an interlocutory injunction). For example the applicant may already have all the relevant evidence, which renders the motion to secure it completely redundant.

As regards industrial property law, as already mentioned, preliminary injunctions in the strict sense of the term have not been regulated at all. One could be under a different impression having read the new provisions of IPL, but this would be a mistake caused by imprecise terminology. The legislator has namely defined information claims as a type of preliminary injunctions securing the claim (which is inconsistent with the Polish legal tradition, as no 'securing' regulation is issued). Apart from this misunderstanding, no special provisions with regard to 'genuine' preliminary injunctions have been enacted. Consequently, in the field of industrial property law only general rules of the CCP apply. Surprisingly, this does not make much of a difference, for the reasons explained above.

Although the general regulation of interlocutory injunctions in the CCP is almost fully consistent with the Enforcement Directive[51] and although because of this fact the necessary implementation of the Directive in this regard required only minor "tweaking" of the existing provisions, the Polish legislator has managed to fail this fairly easy task. "New" special regulations have not been required by the Directive and what was required has not been done. As already mentioned, the problem concerns the possibility of requesting an injunction against persons providing services used in the course of infringement. In the preparatory works[52] in was explained that no special provision was needed since such persons could be qualified as assisting in third party infringements, and thus liable for this assistance on the grounds of Art. 422 CC. This is however incorrect, and even if it were true, the compatibility of the Polish law with the enforcement Directive would be open to doubt. Liability of various service providers, be it in the electronic environment, or a brick & mortar one is a complex legal issue and in this short paper I cannot further pursue it. Suffice it to say that not always is it possible to consider the service provider a person assisting or taking advantage of a third party tort in the meaning of Art. 422 CC.[53] If so, there would be no substantive law claim against such a service provider and consequently no injunction could be obtained. Besides, relying on Art. 422 CC would require to always institute separate legal proceedings on the merits against the service provider, as otherwise the injunction would expire.

51 S. Sołtysiński, A. Nowicka (*supra* note 32), p. 1077.

52 Available at http://bip.mkidn.gov.pl/bip/document/?docId=595.

53 A. Tischner, T. Targosz, *Dostosowanie polskiego prawa własności intelektualnej do wymogów prawa wspólnotowego. Uwagi na tle projektu z dnia 24 maja 2006 r. ustawy o zmianie ustawy o prawie autorskim i prawach pokrewnych oraz o zmianie innych ustaw,* 97 ZNUJ PWPWI 131 (2007).

The most common type of injunction in the Polish court practice are orders to stop putting the infringing goods on the market for the duration of the proceedings. The only doubt Polish courts have had with this type of an injunction is whether it should not be regarded as in fact satisfying the claim, which would render it inadmissible. Presently, the interpretation of the law in force must take account of the Enforcement Directive and the pro community construction of statutes requires that such injunctions be allowed. However, even before the Directive entered into force and Poland became an EU Member State, the courts seem to have solved the problem,[54] maintaining that the claim is not satisfied since the injunction is only temporary (for the duration of court proceedings).[55] The nature of intellectual property disputes often suffices to justify the legal interest required for the injunction. In particular, courts seem to accept the view that damages are difficult to calculate in exact amount and thus the applicant has legal interest in obtaining immediate provisional protection. The most common type of injunction is an order to stop or refrain from alleged infringement. Seizure of infringing goods is often considered too invasive and unnecessary, a view one must have trouble to agree with, especially given how ineffective the enforcement of simple cease orders may be.

It would be premature to conclude that Polish courts have worked out a set of criteria they apply to injunctions with regard to different IP rights. For example it would be too early to conclude that the applicant is more likely to succeed in a trademark case than in a patent case, etc. However, there have been rumours (the decisions have not been published) that in several patent infringement cases concerning generic drugs, where the very question of infringement was open to doubt and would have required comprehensive technical/chemical analysis, injunctions have been denied.

An interesting question poses itself because of the new regime of information rights, which makes it simpler for the prospective plaintiff to calculate damages and assess the likelihood of success in the proceedings on the merits. Logically, this should have an impact on the condition of legal interest (urgency) required by the CCP. If damages can be correctly assessed, the need for an interlocutory decision does not seem so pressing. However, it is not clear whether such reason-

54 See already A. Jakubecki, R. Skubisz (*supra* note 1), p. 106-107.

55 Another "method" is to claim that whenever the court applies Art. 755 CCP, regulating rights and obligations of the parties for the duration of the proceedings, Art. 731 CCP does not apply (Białystok Court of Appeal of 16 September 2009, Case I ACz 739/09, LexPolonica No. 517363, Katowice Court of Appeal of 3 October 2003, Case I ACz 1777/03, Biul.SAKa 2003/4/30). In my opinion this view goes too far and is not necessary to reach the desired goal.

ing is justified under the Enforcement Directive. The Directive requires Members States to provide for both instruments (information rights and preliminary injunctions) and does not treat them as substitutes. On the other hand, the Directive does not require that injunctions be granted automatically whenever an IP infringement is invoked by the applicant. It seems that the balance of interests is inherent in any interlocutory injunction decision and there are no convincing grounds to forgo this principle in IP cases. Granting adequate protection of IP and avoiding over-protection should mean that special rules apply when the nature of IP rights so requires and not simply because the plaintiff brandishes a registration certificate.

The Directive does not directly address a few issues that seem to be important in the Polish court practice. Nevertheless, general principles of Community law, and in particular the principle of effectiveness, should have their say. The first problem comes to play when the defendant is not infringing at the time the decision on the injunction is taken, e.g. has ceased the infringement without acknowledging the plaintiff's rights. Polish courts tend, in my opinion, too generously for the defendant, to conclude that there is no imminent danger of infringement in such cases. It would be however desirable to demand at least an obligation on the part of the infringer to refrain from future infringements, preferably with a penalty clause.

The other problem that may be relevant especially in patent cases deals with the consequences of the expiry of the infringed right in the course of proceedings. Obviously the difficulties may result from the strict character of liability for damages caused by the injunction and the wording of Art. 746 CCP. According to Art. 316 CCP the court has to consider the law and the facts existing on the day the court session preceding the handing down of the judgment is held. Therefore, if the IP right, the infringement of which was pursued by the plaintiff, expires before the final decision is reached (e.g. the patent expires because of the lapse of the 20 year period), the claim must be dismissed to stop infringement. This in turn results in the expiry of the interlocutory injunction, and if read literally, Art. 746 CCP would enable the defendant, who may have been infringing for the whole duration of protection, to sue for damages. Again, this is impossible to accept. The Court of Appeal in Kraków in a very recent judgment[56] stated that damages caused by the injunction cannot be pursued if the defendant would have breached the plaintiff's IP right, as there would have been no *damage* caused by the injunction. The defendant's actions would have been illegal regardless whether the injunction had been issued or not. This, I think, is certainly a correct result, corresponding to the old adage *Nemo auditur propriam turpitu-*

56 Kraków Court of Appeal of 8 December 2009, Case I ACa 906/2009 (unpublished).

dinem allegans. Alternatively, one could invoke the concept of the abuse of right, but the solution proposed by the court seems to be more straightforward.

Because the Polish law is very reluctant towards "piercing the corporate veil", it sometimes happens that the defendants try to circumvent injunctions, using subsidiary companies. Unfortunately, in such a case the plaintiff must institute new proceedings against each subsidiary.

As already mentioned, the two greatest disadvantages of the Polish law with regard to interlocutory injunction are: the factor of time (i.e. injunctions are often granted too late) and the ineffective mechanism of enforcement, especially with regard to cease orders.[57] Both have not been satisfactorily addressed by the statutory amendments implementing the Enforcement Directive. New, shorter time limit in copyright cases is not the answer, since it is the factual time needed to obtain an injunction that matters and not a statutory guideline term. Nothing has been done to ensure effective enforcement of injunctions ordering the defendant to stop the infringement, either. However, at the same time, these weaknesses cannot be confined only to IP cases – on the contrary, they adversely affect all types of proceedings and claims and so the remedy should also be a "general" one.[58]

Conclusions

When one looks at national procedural law concerning interlocutory injunctions in the context of the Enforcement Directive, one may, I think, notice two interesting problems. The first is about the harmonization of laws within the EU and the second about the extent to which IP rights deserve special treatment in civil law proceedings.

Harmonisation of laws in the field not formerly subject to much harmonization and not likely to be subject to comprehensive harmonization in the near future, is certainly a challenge, especially if the harmonisation in question is only partial. The danger looming here is that the EC law may force Member States to adopt solutions alien to their own legal system thus putting its inner logic in danger. Imagine that there is a Member State, whose procedural laws differ greatly from the requirements of the Directive. Such a Member State would still have to enact new provisions for IP cases but it would be difficult to logically justify why interlocutory injunctions in IP cases follow completely different rules than

57 In consequence, one may suspect compliance is based on reputation rather than a fear of sanctions.

58 There are however other views. A. Jakubecki, R. Skubisz (*supra* note 1), p. 94, consider the general regime of procedural law to be inadequate for IP cases.

in other types of cases. Of course, such a Member State could change its whole system of preliminary injunctions to safeguard the coherence of its legal system, but that would be rather a far-fetched conclusion. There is, I believe, no easy answer how to get to reasonable results, but what may help is to grant Member States more leeway as regards implementing Directives regulating only certain aspects of national laws that have not been, nor are immediately intended to be, harmonized.

This leads us neatly to the second question, i.e. whether IP laws deserve special treatment also with regard to purely procedural instruments. I believe that if we agree, the natural goal of procedural laws is to provide effective and fair instruments of enforcing rights and if the national procedural law is sufficiently flexible, the answer should be rather negative.[59] Arguments in favour of special treatment of IP rights,[60] i.e. the facility of infringement, the fact that IP rights should be treated as property rights,[61] or difficulties to correctly assess damages[62] are not unique to IP disputes. The only reason to favour IP rights is the idea that since the rationale of IP is to promote progress and innovation, effective and timely enforcement is essential to achieve this aim. Thus an effective regime of interlocutory injunctions would be required to meet the goals of the IP rights regime in general. There are however some reservations. Although IP rights should be effectively enforced, we should also avoid overprotection since it could in fact have comparable effects to underprotection, constituting an impediment to innovation and development. From this perspective, it would seem, no compelling need exists to award special treatment to IP rights in the regime of interlocutory injunctions. If the regime of interlocutory injunctions is inadequate, then this is a general problem and should be addressed accordingly.

59 S. Sołtysiński, A. Nowicka (*supra* note 32), p. 1080-1081, point out that his could be even unconstitutional since according to Art. 64 (2) of the Polish Constitution property and other economic rights should be protected equally.

60 See e.g. the overview at Ch. Heinze (*supra* note 6), p. 129 et seq.

61 It is interesting to notice that denial of injunctions may practically transform a property rule into a liability rule. On these concepts see G. Calabresi A. D. Melamed, *Property Rules, Liability Rules, and Inalienability: One View of the Cathedral*, 85 Harv. L. Rev. 1089 (1972).

62 T. Dreier, *Kompensation und Prävention – Rechtsfolgen unerlaubter Handlung im Bürgerlichen, Immaterialgüter- und Wettbewerbsrecht,* p. 254 f. (Tübingen 2002).

The Enforcement of Personality Rights

Rüdiger Müller

I. Introduction

Talking about personality rights under the heading "Enforcing Intellectual Property Rights" could have been considered rather provocative in the past. Regarding this question I have the privilege to be able to refer to Professor Götting and his speech given at the conference in Cracow two years ago where he highlighted striking similarities between the economic aspects of personality rights and intellectual property rights.[1]

Intellectual property rights are the object of the Enforcement Directive.[2] Though personality rights are not covered by the directive, I will refer to some provisions of the directive for comparison of the protection of personality rights with that of intellectual property rights in the traditional view from time to time.

Before giving a survey about the relevant causes of action I like to briefly introduce to the personality rights in general under German law. Subsequently the relevant causes of action and the most important remedies with their developments shall be dealt with in detail. Finally I like to address the issue whether personality right protection is provided with the necessary legal instruments or if even an over-enforcement has to be asserted.

II. Personality rights

Firstly it has to be mentioned that there is no provision in German Law that explicitly lays down the requirements and legal consequences of an action under a "general personality right" which is due to the historical development.[3] Only the so called "specific personality rights" are partially codified.

1 Götting, *Personality Rights as Intellectual Property Rights*, in: *Recent Developments in IP Law*, Zeszyty Naukowe Uniwersytetu Jagiellońskiego, Prace Instytutu Prawa Własności Intelektualnej [Works of the Intellectual Property Law Institute], No. 99, 11 (2007).

2 Directive 2004/48/EC of the European Parliament and of the Council of 29 April 2004 on the enforcement of intellectual property rights, OJ EU L 157 of 30 April 2004, p. 45.

3 See Götting in: Götting/Schertz/Seitz (ed.), *Handbuch des Persönlichkeitsrechts*, § 2 (2008); *idem* (*supra* note 1), p. 12 et seq.

1. The specific personality rights

Sec. 22 of the Act on Copyright in Works of Visual Arts (Kunsturheberrechtsgesetz – KUG) from 1907 grants the most important personality right from a practical point of view:[4] the right to one's own image (or portrait). It states that a person's portrait may only be disseminated or exhibited with the consent of the person depicted. Important limitations of this right can be found in the following two sections (Secs. 23, 24 KUG) which seek to reconcile the opposed interests of the portrayed person on the one hand and the public on the other.

With Sec. 12 of the German Civil Code (Bürgerliches Gesetzbuch – BGB) the right to one's name was codified also at the beginning of the 20th century. It protects from the denial and unauthorised use of a person's name. The term "name" is interpreted very broadly. Not only surnames and family names of a person can be covered but also names of legal persons, stage names, pseudonyms or even nicknames.[5]

Furthermore I have to refer to Secs. 12 to 14 of the German Copyright Act (Urheberrechtsgesetz – UrhG). These provisions specify the author's fundamental personality rights (also called "moral rights"), such as the right to first publication, the right to recognition of authorship and the right to integrity of the work. These rights are also counted among the "specific personality rights" but won't be reviewed in the following.

2. The general personality right

It was not before 1954 that the German Federal Court of Justice (Bundesgerichtshof) concluded in one of its judgements[6] that the constitutional rights of the inviolability of human dignity (Art. 1 (1) of the German Constitution (Grundgesetz – GG)) and of the free development of everyone's personality (Art. 2 (1) GG) also required the recognition of a "general personality right" in private law. This "general personality right" found its statutory basis in private law in a provision granting damages (Sec. 823 (1) BGB) as a so called "other [absolute] right" beside the named objects of legal protection that are another person's life, body, health, freedom and property.[7]

4 Götting (*supra* note 1), p. 14.
5 See for further reference Gauss, *German Law*, in: McCarthy, *The Rights of Publicity and Privacy*, Vol. 1, § 6:165, p. 1216 (2nd ed. 2008).
6 BGH 1955 GRUR 197 – *Leserbrief.*
7 Sprau in: Palandt, *Bürgerliches Gesetzbuch*, Sec. 823 marginal note 83 et seq. (69th ed. 2010).

III. Overview of the relevant causes of action

I can just outline the different causes of action which serve as the basis for any discussion on the enforcement of personality rights. Precondition for any claim is of course the violation of one of the rights protected.[8] Further requirements of a successful action will be referred to at each of the claims mentioned.

1. Claims concerning the abatement of the interference

a. Prohibitory injunctions

It is only the right to one's name that statutory law expressively provides an entitlement to injunctive relief.[9] Neither for the right to one's image nor for the general personality right a similar provision can be found. However, the courts apply Sec. 1004 (1) 2 BGB. This section actually provides injunctive relief only in the case of the interference of property. Nevertheless it is applied by analogy to the infringement of the other absolute rights mentioned in Sec. 823 BGB, therefore also for violations of personality rights.[10] The application by analogy is acknowledged because there is an unintentional gap in statutory law and the balance of interests behind the provision is comparable to the situation which is not covered by the written preconditions.[11]

Granting a prohibitory injunction moreover requires a danger of further interferences or – if there hasn't been any interference so far – an imminent danger of a violation.[12] Additionally the claimant must not be under an obligation to tolerate the interference. However, proof of fault is not necessary.[13]

A parallel provision protecting intellectual property rights can be found in Art. 11 Enforcement Directive which allows an injunction aimed at prohibiting the continuation of the infringement.

8 See on this Beverly-Smith/Ohly/Lucas-Schloetter, *Privacy, Property and Personality*, p. 105-119 (2005).

9 Sec. 12 clause 2 BGB.

10 Bassenge in: Palandt, *Bürgerliches Gesetzbuch*, Sec. 1004 marginal note 4 (69th ed. 2010).

11 Cf. Bassenge (*supra* note 10), Sec. 1004 marginal note 4; see also Sprau (*supra* note 7), marginal notes 48, 55 et seq. before Sec. 1.

12 Bassenge (*supra* note 10), Sec. 1004 marginal note 32.

13 Bassenge (*supra* note 10), Sec. 1004 marginal note 34 et seq.

b. Removal of the interference; correction and revocation

Sec. 1004 BGB applied by analogy also provides an order for removal of the interference under the same conditions as the prohibitory injunction.[14] In contrast, danger of further interferences or an imminent danger of interference is not required.

By applying Sec. 1004 BGB case law also grants a claim for correction or revocation of a demonstrably false factual statement.[15] The correction has to be made in the same manner as the statement itself. It must have the same form regarding position and size for example if it has been published in a magazine.[16]

These claims may be compared with Art. 10 Enforcement Directive. However, the corrective measures mentioned only apply to goods, their materials and manufacturing implements.

c. Counter-statements

Though talking about civil enforcement let me throw a short glance at a claim under public law which also deals with the abatement of interference in the broader sense. Sec. 10 of the Saxon Media Law Statute provides a claim for a counter-statement regarding publications in Saxony. It concerns a statement of the claimant which is published in his own name and has to be reported completely and literally in the defendant's print work provided it meets the requirements of Sec. 10. Mainly, the counter-statement has to refer to an allegation of facts and has to contain facts itself rather than opinions. As public Media Law falls into the legislative authority of the federal states there are slightly different provisions in each one of them.[17]

d. Supplementary claims

Within the scope of Sec. 1004 BGB supplementary claims can be granted. Removal of the interference in terms of the elimination of any consequential effects[18] may also include the publication of the judgement[19] or even the destruc-

14 Sec. 1004 (1) 1 BGB.
15 BGH 1995 GRUR 224 – *Erfundenes Exclusiv-Interview/Caroline von Monaco I.*
16 BGH 1995 GRUR 224 – *Erfundenes Exclusiv-Interview/Caroline von Monaco I.*
17 For further references see Seitz in: Götting/Schertz/Seitz (ed.), *Handbuch des Persönlichkeitsrechts*, § 48 (2008).
18 "Folgenbeseitigungsanspruch".

tion of infringing copies.[20] A successful claimant is also entitled to demand from the infringer to hand over all violating copies instead of destroying them.[21] Special provisions of the Act on Copyright in Works of Visual Arts are applicable for the two latter claims if the right to one's own image is concerned.[22]

Another supplementary claim deals with the discovery regarding the content and extent of the unauthorised use,[23] for example the quantity of the infringing copies sold. The claim is based on Sec. 242 BGB, a very broad provision about acting in accordance with "good faith" if performing contractual obligations. This section is known as a so called "general clause" and it provides a basis for the development of case law. Discovery in terms of a right of information requires that the defendant is already held liable for injunctive relief or damages as the burden of proof in general has to remain on the claimant.[24] Further preconditions are that the plaintiff's lack of knowledge is not his fault and that he is unable to gain the information in a different way. Finally it must not be difficult for the defendant to provide the information. The interests of the parties involved have to be balanced as well.

Apart from the right of information especially regarding damages, the supplementary claims mentioned are more or less of minor significance in practice. The Enforcement Directive grants similar rights, for example in Art. 8 the right of information, in Art. 10 (1) lit. c) destruction as a corrective measure and in Art. 15 the publication of judicial decisions.

e. Interlocutory injunctions

In order to trigger a quick and effective reaction to the violation of personality rights the grant of an interlocutory injunction[25] is vital. An application is successful if – after a summary assessment – the court concludes that the claim is well-founded and the injunction is necessary to prevent a significant detriment.[26] The applicant does not have to prove the requirements fully but only has to show

19 See on this Freund in: Götting/Schertz/Seitz (ed.), *Handbuch des Persönlichkeitsrechts*, § 53 marginal notes 47-71 (2008), with further references.
20 Cf. Freund (*supra* note 19), § 53 marginal notes 77-81.
21 Cf. Freund (*supra* note 19), § 53 marginal notes 87-93.
22 See Sec. 37 and Sec. 38 KUG.
23 "Auskunftsanspruch".
24 See on this and the following Freund (*supra* note 19), § 53 marginal notes 1-46.
25 Cf. Secs. 935 and 940 German Code of Civil Procedure (Zivilprozessordnung – ZPO).
26 Beverly-Smith/Ohly/Lucas-Schloetter (*supra* note 8), p. 139; see on interlocutory injunctions Spangler in: Götting/Schertz/Seitz (ed.), *Handbuch des Persönlichkeitsrechts*, § 55 (2008).

them credibly.[27] Intellectual property rights are protected in the same manner by Art. 9 (1) lit. a) Enforcement Directive.

2. Claims for compensation in the broader sense

a. Damages

The most relevant provision granting damages in tort law is Sec. 823 BGB. As already mentioned it protects another person's life, body, health, freedom, property or any other right. According to case law, the latter one includes not only the so called "specific personality rights" but also the "general personality right". This cause of action requires fault on the part of the defendant which means that he has acted either intentionally or negligently. Whenever the defendant knows that he is exploiting a personality aspect without the person's permission, he will regularly act intentionally. Negligence is defined as a lack of reasonable (or usually required) care,[28] for example in cases involving false press information. Damages are of course also granted if intellectual property rights are violated, according to Art. 13 Enforcement Directive.

b. Unjust enrichment

With Sec. 812 BGB German law also provides a general action for unjust enrichment. According to this claim anyone who obtains a benefit at another person's expense without legal cause is obliged to surrender this benefit to the other person. In case the benefit cannot be transferred in nature the defendant must pay an amount of money representing the value of the benefit in compensation.[29] Alongside the immaterial interests German courts also recognise the commercial aspects of personality rights.[30] Therefore this action is applicable if the legal position encroached indeed attributes commercial benefits to its holder. This question has to be answered in each particular case. An important advantage over the claim for damages according to Sec. 823 BGB is that the action for unjust enrichment does not require any fault on the part of the defendant.

27 "Glaubhaftmachung"; cf. Sec. 294 ZPO.
28 Sec. 276 (2) BGB.
29 Cf. Sec. 818 (2) BGB.
30 BGH 1956 GRUR 427, 430 – *Paul Dahlke*.

c. Compensation for non-pecuniary damage (*solatium*)

To grant compensation for non-pecuniary damage in personality right cases the courts today directly refer to Art. 1 GG (inviolability of human dignity) and Art. 2 (1) GG (free development of everyone's personality). Since these articles require private law to grant effective protection of the personality and since this protection remains deficient if it only provides compensation for economic loss, private law has to allow the award of solatium.[31] Therefore the causes of action for solatium in the traditional view (now Sec. 253 BGB) does not preclude compensation for non-pecuniary damage in personality right cases even though this kind of legal position is not part of the exclusively named rights.[32]

Preconditions for such a claim are a serious infringement of the personality right and that the violation cannot be compensated in other ways like correction or revocation for example.[33] Furthermore the defendant must have acted unlawfully and with fault as this action is based on tort law. The question of the seriousness of the infringement depends on the extent and manner of the violation and on other circumstances of each case like the questions whether the private sphere has been violated, whether there have been cases of libel and slander or whether the claimant was mocked in the eyes of the public. In addition the degree of negligence on the part of the defendant may be decisive.[34]

The provisions about damages in the course of the Enforcement Directive also grant compensation for immaterial loss in appropriate cases as regulated in Art. 13 (1) lit. a).

IV. The most relevant remedies and their development in case law

After pointing out the causes of action I now like to draw your attention to the outcome – the actual remedies. I will talk about the most important remedies more detailed and will also have a look at their development in case law.

31 BGH 1962 GRUR 105 et seq. – *Ginsengwurzel;* BGH 1995 GRUR 224, 229 – *Erfundenes Exclusiv-Interview/Caroline von Monaco I.*

32 Cf. Müller in: Götting/Schertz/Seitz (ed.), *Handbuch des Persönlichkeitsrechts*, § 51 marginal notes 1-6 (2008).

33 See on the requirements *supra* note 31 and Müller (*supra* note 32), § 51 marginal notes 11-29.

34 Cf. Gauss (*supra* note 5), § 6:169, p. 1223.

1. Injunctive relief

Beside the removal of the interference prohibitory injunctions are very important for the right holders, especially in cases of a continuous infringement, for example if an allegation is sustained or a violating picture is kept on a website. However, it is pretty easy for the defendant to escape this remedy if he is not interested in continuing the infringement because he has for example already sold enough copies of a magazine containing infringing articles or pictures. He only has to provide a declaration to cease and desist[35] in order to eliminate the danger of further interferences, which is a precondition of the claim. At this point it becomes apparent that injunctive relief as a sole remedy is often not very effective; according to the principle: Infringing in the first place and refraining from any further violation afterwards.[36]

In addition there is no protection against reporting in substantially the same manner of an infringing report[37] as each specific case must be decided for its own. Therefore publishing a picture can establish a claim in a certain context and it might be justified to publish the same picture in other circumstances. Recently the Federal Court of Justice held that the children of the well-known former football player and coach Franz Beckenbauer are not granted prohibitory injunctions regarding the publication of their portraits in general, notwithstanding the fact that they are still minors.[38] There court stated that there might be situations in which a justification of the publication is justified.

2. Damages

The general rule for the assessment of damages is that the claimant must be put into the position in which he would have been, had the damaging act not occurred.[39] Usually the damage is evaluated by a precise assessment of all losses suffered because of the violation. As the unauthorised exploitation of personality aspects is comparable to the infringement of intellectual property rights, it is acknowledged that the claimant can also ask for damages calculated on the basis of a reasonable licence fee or on the basis of the profits made by the defendant in

35 "Strafbewehrte Unterlassungserklärung"; see on this v. Hutten in: Götting/Schertz/Seitz (ed.), *Handbuch des Persönlichkeitsrechts*, § 47 marginal notes 38-49 (2008).

36 Cf. Götting, LMK (Kommentierte BGH-Rechtsprechung Lindenmaier-Möhring/beck-fachdienst Zivilrecht) 2006, 172015, para. 3.

37 BGH 2008 GRUR 446 – *Kerngleiche Berichterstattung;* BGH 2009 GRUR 1091 – *Wilde Frisur des Andrea Casiraghi.*

38 BGH 2010 GRUR 173 – Kinder von Franz Beckenbauer.

39 Sec. 249 (1) BGB.

the course of the violation.[40] These methods of assessing damages are provided because it is often difficult to establish evidence of a substantial loss. In case of the infringement of an intellectual property right the same methods apply under certain conditions according to Art. 13 Enforcement Directive.

The "reasonable licence approach" was primarily applied in cases of unauthorised advertisements with celebrities.[41] In the past, for using this method case law required the claimant to have been able and willing to grant a licence for the particular act, which was usually denied in cases where only non-material aspects like honour and good reputation were infringed.[42] The courts argued that such a claim would otherwise imply that a person whose personality rights had been infringed would be prepared to give permission to the humiliating exploitation of his personality for a certain amount of money. This assumption would result in a further violation of the personality right.[43] This finding was broadly criticised[44] because the "reasonable licence approach" is a hypothetical device and does therefore not require the implication of a subjective intention to grant licences. Even worse, courts refused an appropriate compensation in the most serious cases of personality right infringement.

The critical commentators however had to wait until the year 2006 when the case of the former minister of finance Oskar Lafontaine was decided.[45] The judgement was mainly welcomed. It concerned the unauthorised use of Oskar Lafontaine's image in an advertising campaign of a car rental company shortly after his resignation from the government. The Federal Court of Justice reversed its long standing ruling and held that the award of reasonable licence fees does not depend on the ability and willingness of the right holder to give his consent. However since this decision there has been no case where a court granted reasonable licence fees to claimants whose personality aspects have not been of a noticeable commercial value so far.

The amounts awarded are dependent on the defendant's commercial benefit. Therefore the sums may differ considerably from case to case. Just for illustration I like to mention two cases about well known persons whose pictures had

40 Beverly-Smith/Ohly/Lucas-Schloetter (*supra* note 8), p. 142-143.

41 BGH 1956 GRUR 427, 429 – *Paul Dahlke;* BGH 1987 GRUR 128, 129 – NENA; BGH 1992 GRUR 557, 558 – *Talkmaster-Foto.*

42 BGH 1958 GRUR 408 – *Herrenreiter;* BGH 1959 GRUR 430, 433 – *Caterina Valente;* BGH 1962 GRUR 105, 106 – *Ginsengwurzel.*

43 BGH 1958 GRUR 408, 409 – *Herrenreiter.*

44 Götting, *Persönlichkeitsrechte als Vermögensrechte*, p. 50 et seq. (1995), with further references at p. 53 note 199; idem, *Sanktionen bei Verletzung des postmortalen Persönlichkeitsrechts*, 2004 GRUR 801, 803; Beuthien/Schmölz, *Persönlichkeitsschutz durch Persönlichkeitsgüterrechte*, p. 41 et seq. (1999); Däubler, *Anspruch auf Lizenzgebühr und Herausgabe des Verletzergewinns*, 1969 JuS 49, 51 et seq.

45 BGH 2007 GRUR 139 – *Rücktritt des Finanzministers.*

been used for advertising the introduction of a new kind of newspaper. In the first case a picture of the former tennis player Boris Becker was used without consent as part of a dummy front page of the newspaper in a very large campaign. There was no editorial content going along with the picture. The claimant was granted the very high amount of 1.2 million EUR.[46] The second case involved the former foreign minister Joschka Fischer. His portrait with the features of a young child was also used without consent but he was granted "only" 200 000 EUR.[47]

3. Unjust enrichment

As already mentioned the main advantage of a claim for unjust enrichment is that no fault at all is required. However this remedy is limited to the objective value of the benefit obtained as stated in Sec. 818 (2) BGB. This value of the benefit is equivalent to the amount of a reasonable licence fee.[48] Therefore the same principles apply as mentioned above.

4. Compensation for non-pecuniary damage

Courts appear to be rather reluctant to grant compensation for non-pecuniary damage. Particularly the question of the seriousness of the infringement is often answered in the negative. The courts' reluctance becomes more understandable when we look back to the roots of this claim. Due to the very restrictive wording of the former provision on solatium,[49] courts had to "create" a new (and unwritten) claim as a so called last resort ("*ultima ratio*") following the intention of Art. 1 and 2 GG.[50]

The first attempt of the Federal Court of Justice to establish such an action by applying the very restrictive provision on solatium by analogy was broadly criticised not for the outcome itself but because of the reasoning.[51] In this so called

46 Munich District Court I 2006 AfP 382; repealed by the BGH as far as the period was concerned in which the publishing company was unable or could not reasonably be expected to use the cover of an already published issue, see 2010 GRUR 546 – *Der strauchelnde Liebling.*

47 Hamburg District Court 2007 GRUR 143 – *Lizenzgebühr für Joschka Fischer.*

48 BGH 1956 GRUR 427, 429 et seq. – *Paul Dahlke.*

49 Cf. the old version of Sec. 847 BGB which was replaced by Sec. 253 (2) BGB in 2002.

50 BGH 1962 GRUR 105, 106 et seq. – *Ginsengwurzel.*

51 Cf. Beverly-Smith/Ohly/Lucas-Schloetter (*supra* note 8), p. 144 et seq.

"gentleman rider" case[52] from 1958 the picture of a brewery owner showing him on a horse during a riding contest was published in an advertisement for a sexual stimulant. The claimant was granted about 5 000 EUR in compensation for non-pecuniary damage.

During the following years courts did not very often award more than the amount obtained in this leading case. A sum equivalent to about 7 500 EUR was granted to a princess because of the publication of a completely fictitious interview.[53] A sum of around 25 000 EUR was awarded to the owner of a department store chain who was grossly negligently alleged by a news magazine to have offered 6 million D-Mark to members of German parliament in order to influence their voting.[54] The fact that the allegation had only based on an anonymous document was especially taken into consideration. In this case the court did not only stress the purpose of giving satisfaction to the claimant but also took into account the defendant's commercial interest in the publication. Nevertheless these rather high amounts remained very exceptional.[55]

In 1994 a very important judgement was handed down with the case of a fictitious interview with another princess, Caroline of Monaco (later married: Caroline of Hannover).[56] She was and still is writing legal history with her cases. Caroline refused to give an interview at her holiday resort saying "I don't give any interviews." The defendant turned this sentence into a detailed "exclusive interview" in one of his magazines. The would-be interview was about Caroline's private life and her wanting to be let alone. Two months later the defendant continued his pretended "report" by publishing pictures taken by a paparazzi alleging they came from Caroline's family album. Eventually he published an article alleging her intention to marry pretty soon. A photo composition showing her in a wedding dress next to her boyfriend accompanied the article. The court granted a compensation of approximately 90 000 EUR.

Beside the fact that the amount granted was higher than ever before in personality right cases, the reasons of the decision were ground-breaking.[57] The Federal Court of Justice highlighted the function of compensation for non-pecuniary damage in such cases. The primary purpose of giving satisfaction to the claimant is now supplemented by the purpose of preventing further infringements. Without an adequate amount of compensation the claimant would be helplessly sub-

52 BGH 1958 GRUR 408 – *Herrenreiter.*

53 BGH 1965 GRUR 254 – *Exklusiv-Interview/Soraya.*

54 BGH *1977 GRUR 674 – Abgeordnetenbestechung.*

55 Cf. Burkhardt in: Wenzel, *Das Recht der Wort- und Bildberichterstattung*, Ch. 14 marginal note 149 (5th ed. 2003).

56 BGH 1995 GRUR 224 – *Erfundenes Exclusiv-Interview/Caroline von Monaco I.*

57 See on the following BGH 1995 GRUR 224, 228 et seq. – *Erfundenes Exclusiv-Interview/Caroline von Monaco I.*

jected to a ruthless and forcible commercial exploitation of her personality. The preventive function results from the need to protect the personality right effectively. The amount granted has to be noticeable on the defendant's part and has to lead to an effect of obstruction. On the other hand the sum must not impose an excessive restriction on the freedom of press. Further, the basis of assessment has to consist of the defendant's profits made in the course of the infringement. However the claimant is not entitled to cream off the profits itself. Matters of effectiveness and prevention referred to in the judgement can also be found in the general provisions of the Enforcement Directive, namely in Art. 3 (2).

Subsequently the courts granted significantly higher amounts of compensation for non-pecuniary damage than they used to in personality right cases. In another case concerning Princess Caroline she was awarded the sum of about 100 000 EUR after pictures of her had been published which were taken while she was praying in a church and relaxing on an isolated boat rather away from the shore.[58]

Caroline's daughter Alexandra obtained a compensation of about 75 000 EUR in a further case because of the publication of paparazzi pictures taken on her way home from the clinic shortly after her birth and in other private situations with her parents.[59]

Another case concerned the German writer Hera Lind and her children who were also granted about 75 000 EUR in compensation.[60] Again it was a paparazzi who took pictures of them namely at a hidden part of a beach. Some of the photographs showed the writer naked and such a picture was printed on the front page of the infringing magazine.

Lastly I like to mention the case of a 16-year old girl who was the victim of a well-known TV presenter who repeatedly made fun of her because of a video clip in which she introduced herself by mentioning her name and age.[61] Her name gave cause for persistent mocking by the TV presenter. Finally he associated her with porn industry and considered her suited for this kind of business. The court held that his conduct was not covered by the freedom of art and sentenced him to pay a compensation of 70 000 EUR.

58 Hamburg Court of Appeal 2001 OLGR Hamburg 139.

59 BGH 2005 GRUR 179 – *Tochter von Caroline von Hannover.*

60 Hamburg District Court 2002 ZUM 68.

61 Hamm Court of Appeal 2004 GRUR 970 – *TV Total.*

5. Post-mortem protection and its limitations

Finally I like to talk briefly about the post-mortem protection of personality rights and its limitations. The right to one's own picture provides that the portrait of a person may only be published with the consent of the deceased person's relatives for 10 years after the death of the depicted person.[62] If the right to one's name or the general personality right is concerned courts distinguish between commercial use and the immaterial aspects. The courts used to provide post-mortem protection only in cases in which honour, good reputation or other non-material aspects of personality were infringed because the constitutional guarantee of the free development of everyone's personality[63] was not held to be applicable post-mortem.[64]

In the year 1999 the Federal Court of Justice reversed this rule in the "Marlene Dietrich" decision by stating that claims for damages may well be transferred to the heirs of the deceased right holder as such transfer is necessary to protect her from the unauthorised commercial use.[65] Marlene Dietrich's name and pictures had been used in an advertisement and merchandise without the consent of her heirs. Here the formula applies: "Protection against commercialisation by means of commercialisation."[66]

However this ruling does not help in cases in which the deceased is not held to have commercial interest as he or she for example was not known to the public at the time of infringement. This was ruled in a case of a murdered woman who was filmed by a TV magazine crew just after the crime took place and was showed in the TV programme.[67] This decision was criticised[68] as here again it becomes obvious that prohibitory injunctions on their own are not very effective remedies at all. Furthermore a claim for compensation for non-pecuniary damage is not applicable if only ideal aspects of personality are concerned because a deceased is not able anymore to receive satisfaction.[69]

For a long time there was no strict limitation period for the post-mortem protection apart from the 10 years after the death of the holder of a right to his own picture. The general rule is that the duration of protection depends on the cir-

62 Sec. 22 clause 3 KUG.
63 Art. 2 GG.
64 BGH 1971 GRUR 461 – *Mephisto;* see also Gauss (*supra* note 5), § 6:167, p. 1218 et seq.
65 BGH 2000 GRUR 709 – *Marlene Dietrich.*
66 Cf. Götting (*supra* note 36), para. 2c.
67 BGH 2006 GRUR 252 – *Postmortaler Persönlichkeitsschutz.*
68 Götting (*supra* note 36), paras. 2b, 2c, 3.
69 BGH 2006 GRUR 252, 254 – *Postmortaler Persönlichkeitsschutz;* consenting Götting (*supra* note 36), para. 2a.

cumstances of the specific case. The protection decreases at the rate at which the image of the right holder "fades in the eyes of the public".[70]

However, a highly criticised[71] judgement of the Federal Court of Justice recently limited all claims based on the infringement of the post-mortem protection concerning the unauthorised commercial use to a period of 10 years after the death of the deceased.[72] The court applied the limitation of the right to one's own image by analogy but also stressed that the protection of the ideal parts of personality rights is not covered by this restriction.

V. Conclusions

Does German law already provide the instruments necessary for an adequate protection of personality rights? Where are the gaps of protection, what changes have to be proposed?

Let us first have a look at the damages and unjust enrichment respectively. It has been suggested to apply the claim for reasonable licence fees also in cases of – up to the infringement – unknown persons who could not claim a particular commercial value of their personality aspects so far.[73] In my opinion this would be clearly a further step towards an adequate protection of personality rights. On the other hand I fear it might be rather challenging to assess the sum of money representing the value of the defendant's benefit in some cases. What, for example, would the heirs of the murdered woman mentioned before have reasonably demanded for the consent to film the scene just after the murder took place? Of course within the claim for unjust enrichment one should only look at the benefit gained by the infringer rather than any economic loss on the part of the claimant. But still, it sounds pretty odd to me to ask for the "reasonable" licence fee in such a case.

The sums granted for claims for compensation for non-pecuniary damage are still not high enough to protect from persistent violations.[74] The courts do not get tired to stress that solatium has nothing to do with punitive damages even though

70 BGH 1995 GRUR 668 – *Emil Nolde;* see also Gauss (*supra* note 5), § 6:167, p. 1219 et seq.

71 Götting, 2007 GRUR 170 et seq. (comment on BGH 2007 GRUR 168 – *kinski-klaus.de*); Reber, *Die Schutzdauer des postmortalen Persönlichkeitsrechts in Deutschland und den USA*, 2007 GRUR Int. 492, 494 et seq.

72 BGH 2007 GRUR 168 – *kinski-klaus.de.*

73 Cf. Götting (*supra* note 36), paras. 2b, 2c.

74 For a critical comment regarding the (comparatively little) sums of solatium according to Sec. 253 (2) BGB e. g. in case of rape see Neumeyer, *Schmerz, Kommerz, Frau mit Herz*, 2009 AfP 465.

its purpose is also to prevent further infringements. In German law punitive damages would conflict with the constitutional guarantees granted to the accused in criminal law proceedings.[75] But if we have a look at the defendants such as well-earning big publishing companies or TV production companies or for example at the continuous infringement of princess Caroline's rights in spite of the many previous decisions, one may doubt the effectiveness of the verdicts. The issue of effectiveness is also important in the course of the intellectual property rights as mentioned in Art. 3 (2) Enforcement Directive.

Regarding the protection post mortem the limitation concerning the unauthorised commercial use up to a period of 10 years after the death appears to be far too restrictive. One can only hope that the courts will be willing to listen to the commentators and will not adhere to their current position for too long.

Do we have to worry about an over-enforcement when contemplating personality right protection? The answer of course depends on our own attitude. Are we generally more in favour of the freedom of press and opinion or in favour of the free development of the personality? Without doubt the opposing interests always have to be considered. However providing more precise claims and more effective remedies for the protection of personality rights would certainly not lead to the death of the freedom of press because the balance of interests always has to remain the instrument to ensure justness in each individual case.

75 Beverly-Smith/Ohly/Lucas-Schloetter (*supra* note 8), p. 146.

The Compulsory License under Competition Law

Michał du Vall

At a 2007 Kraków conference at the Institute for the Intellectual Property Law of the Jagiellonian University a paper co-authored by Mrs. Jeannette Viniol and me was presented. The title of that paper was *Abuse of Patent Rights under Anti-trust law*[1] and the following presentation is an elaboration on the same subject.

I. *International compulsory license regulations*

Art. 5 of the Paris Convention for the Protection of Industrial Property of 1883 provides for the possibility of granting compulsory licenses in the case of protected inventions and utility models. It also stipulates that in three years from the date of a patent grant or four years from the date of a patent application, a compulsory license cannot be obtained due to non-use of the invention.

In the Trade-Related Aspects of Intellectual Property Rights (TRIPS) Agreement we find detailed rules concerning compulsory patent licenses (Art. 31). At the same time Art. 21 of the Agreement is an *expressis verbis* exclusion of granting compulsory licenses for trade marks. The agreement also concerns anti-trust practices in contractual licenses. Namely, according to Art. 40 of the Agreement, 'members agree that some licensing practices or conditions pertaining to intellectual property rights which restrain competition may have adverse effects on trade and may adversely affect the transfer and dissemination of technology' (para. 1) and that 'nothing in this Agreement shall prevent Members from specifying in their legislation licensing practices or conditions that may in particular cases constitute an abuse of intellectual property rights having an adverse effect on competition in the relevant market' (para. 2).

As can be seen Art. 40 of the Agreement do not limit the possible control of license agreements to just patent licenses and abuse of a dominant position, therefore they can cover the whole subject-matter of protection (i.e. works in the meaning of copyright law, industrial designs, etc.).

1 J. Viniol, M. du Vall, *Abuse of Patent Rights under Anti-trust law*, in: *Recent Developments in IP Law*, Zeszyty Naukowe Uniwersytetu Jagiellońskiego, Prace Instytutu Prawa Własności Intelektualnej (Works of the Intellectual Property Law Institute) Vol. 99 (2007), p. 81.

II. The possibility to grant compulsory licenses based on the provisions of the anti-trust law

1. Introduction

Generally speaking, an excessively concentrated market has an adverse effect on competition. The statement is not always true with regard to innovations. Depending on the type of innovations, an excessive concentration of the market and the concomitant market power, may be or may not be favourable for innovation.[2] On the one hand, competition necessitates the introduction of better products onto the market; on the other hand, when innovations require considerable investments (as in pharmaceutical industry), a high degree of concentration actually enables these investments. It must be remembered then that competition is not an end in itself but a means to an end, which is launching new (innovative) products, the increase of production, the improvement of its quality, and the lowering of prices.[3]

The overall economic and social goals of the intellectual property rights (IPRs) and the anti-trust law coincide: they help bring benefits to consumers and contribute to an effective allocation of the means of production.[4] It is the paradigm of the anti-trust law that competition of undertakings is a driving force of economy, by giving, among other things, the strong impetus to innovation, which in turn is the basis of economic development.[5] With effective competition, consumers have better products of the best possible quality, at the lowest prices. IPRs are also thought to realize these goals since, by a guaranteed legal exclusivity, they encourage to invest in research and development.[6] The two areas complement each other.[7] It was aptly said in the doctrine that it is no coincidence that

2 Cf. I. Haracoglou, *Anti-trust law and Patents. A Follow-on Innovation Perspective in the Biopharmaceutical Industry*, p. 126 and notes 17-20 (Cheltenham, Northampton, 2008).

3 Cf. J. Temple Lang, *Compulsory Licensing of Intellectual Property in European Community Antitrust Law,* p. 17 (2002), available at: http://www.ftc.gov/opp/intellect/020522 langdoc.pdf.

4 Cf. para. 7 Commission Notice: Guidelines on the Application of Art. 81 of the EC Treaty to Technology Transfer Agreements, OJ EC C 101 of 27 April 2004, p. 2 (later Guidance 2004), and M. Dolmans, A. Piilola, *The Proposed New Technology Transfer Block Exemption – Is Europe really better off than with the current regulation?*, (2003) World Competition 26 (4), 541, 543.

5 Cf. R. J. Gilbert, W. K. Tom, *Is Innovation King at the Antitrust Agencies? The Intellectual Property Guidelines Five Years Later*, 69 Antitrust Law Journal 45 (2001).

6 *L.c.* and notes 9 and 10 therein.

7 Cf. M. Dolmans, A. Piilola (*supra* note 4), p. 543, and para. 5 of the preamble of the Commission Regulation (EC) No. 772/2004 and para. 7 of Guidance 2004. In former works and case-law the stress was put on the conflict of the two protection regimes; cf. e.g. D. G. Goyder, *EC Anti-trust law*, p. 253 (Oxford 1990). Also see para. 7 of Guidance

The Parliament of England's Statute of Monopolies introduced in the seventeenth century is both the first legal act providing rules on monopoly and competition control, and the first patent law in Britain by which patent exclusivity was granted for the most important exception from the provisions.[8] Also today IP protection is considered as an exception from the rule of free competition.[9] However, the means used by the two legal domains are completely different: patent law grants legally determined exclusive rights (that is monopoly) to the right holder to use the invention while the anti-trust law governs the transactions providing for the parties involved and the third parties, a number of restrictions (such as territorial restrictions) and the behaviour of the undertakings that dominate the market. Hence the complicated relations linking these domains often manifest themselves in a different judgement of the behaviour of the exclusive rights holders.[10]

Considering the relation between the norms of the anti-trust law and IPRs, it must be said that the anti-trust law has 'priority' insofar as IPRs cannot substantiate abuse of the anti-trust law.[11] Authors writing on the subject point out in this context that the priority of the anti-trust law principles stems from its key role in the EC legal system and, secondarily, from the fact that they are norms of the public law whereas IPRs are private property rights.[12]

The EC anti-trust law does not encroach upon the system of granting exclusive rights by member states[13] and the very existence of such rights. As a rule, the EC law does not interfere with the normal exercise of IPR – including full insurance that the rights are observed[14] and the rejection of a license even if the

2004; M. Dolmans, A. Piilola (*supra* note 4); M. Monti, *The New EU Policy on Technology Transfer Agreement*, European Commission Press Release of 16 January 2004, Speach 04/19, p. 1.

8 Cf. F.-K. Beier, *Wettbewerbsfreiheit und Patentschutz,* 1978 GRUR 126; J. Viniol, *Some Thoughts Regarding the Use and Abuse of Patent Rights under Art. 82 EC Treaty and under German Monopoly Law*, in: J. Viniol, M. du Vall (*supra* note 1), p. 84. See also D. Miąsik, *Reguła rozsądku w prawie antymonopolowym. Studium prawnoporównawcze*, p. 25 et seqq. (Kraków 2004).

9 Cf. B. Kramer, *Patentschutz und Zugang zu Medikamenten. Rechtliche und ökonomische Implikation*, p. 98 et seq. (Cologne *et al.* 2007).

10 Cf. E. Elhauge, D. Geradin, *Global Anti-trust law and Economics*, p. 191 et seqq. (Oxford 2007).

11 Cf. U.S. Court of Appeals for the District of Columbia Circuit 253 F.3d 34 (D.C. Cir. 2001) 62 et seq. – *US v. Microsoft.*

12 S. Anderman, *Does the Microsoft Case offer a New Paradigm for the 'Exceptional Circumstances' Test and Compulsory Copyright Licenses under EC Anti-trust law?*, (2004) 1(2) CompLRev 1, 21.

13 Cf. joined Cases C-241/91 P and C-242/91 P, ECR 1995, I-743 – *RTE and ITP v. Commission.*

14 Cf. Case 53/87, ECR 1988, 6039 – *Maxicar v. Renault.*

right holder has a dominant market position.[15] As highlighted by the ECJ, intellectual property rights – like any object of property – must be regarded as more or less worthless without the guaranteed rights to exercise them.[16] Notwithstanding this, the ECJ showed that some forms of the exercise of the exclusive rights may abuse the EC law, namely the principle of the free movement of goods.[17] The vague difference between 'existence' and 'exercise' of IPRs has been criticized.[18] In its later decisions, the ECJ tried to reduce the state of legal uncertainty resulting from the admissibility of the interference of the anti-trust law in the unspecified form of the 'exercise' of the law, emphasizing that it is (relatively) 'safe' to use IPRs within their specific subject-matter.[19] From that point of view, it is basically legal to disallow third parties to use the subject-matter of the right for economic purposes[20] because such is the nature of all exclusive rights – they exist exactly for the purpose of safeguarding the subject-matter from competi-

15 Case C-418/01, ECR 2004, 5039 – *IMS Health GmbH & Co. v. OHG/NDC Health GmbH & Co.* ("The refusal to grant a license, even if it is the act of an undertaking holding a dominant position, cannot in itself constitute an abuse of a dominant position").

16 See J. Viniol (*supra* notes 8 and 1), p. 86.

17 The distinction between 'existence' and 'exercise' of exclusive rights was made by the ECJ: Judgment of the Court of 13 July 1966, joined Cases C-56/64 und 58/64, ECR 1966, 299 – *Grundig & Consten v. Commission*. In Poland the distinction was applied in a normative act, namely in Art. 2 of the act on competition and consumer protection of 16 February 2007, "Dziennik Ustaw" (Journal of Laws of the Republic of Poland) 2007, No. 50, para. 331:
1. The Act is without prejudice to the rights vested pursuant to the provisions concerning protection of intellectual and industrial property rights, in particular the provisions on the protection of inventions, utility model and industrial rights, topography of integrated circuits, trade marks, geographical indications, copyright and rights related to copyright.
2. The Act applies to the concluded between undertakings: 1) agreements, in particular license agreements, as well as to other practices of exercising rights referred to in Paragraph 1; 2) agreements concerning information undisclosed to the general public, related to: a) technical or technological information, b) rules of organisation and management - in relation to which steps were taken in order to prevent their disclosure, where such agreements result in an unjustified limitation of freedom of business activity of the parties, or in a significant restriction of competition within the market.
Clearly the quoted act is based on the traditional distinction between 'existence' and 'exercise' of exclusive rights.

18 A. Ch. Beunen, *Protection for databases: the European Database Directive and its effects in the Netherlands, France and the United Kingdom*, Nijmegen 2007, p. 236, note 16; V. Korah, *An Introduction Guide to EC Anti-trust law and Practice*, 8th ed., Oxford 2004, p. 292.

19 Cf. J. Viniol (*supra* notes 8 and 1), p. 86 and decisions referred to in note 19. It must be said that the 'specific subject-matter' doctrine was developed in the context of the free movement of goods expressed in Art. 30 ECT (now Art. 36 TFEU) and not in Art. 82 ECT (now Art. 102 TFEU).

20 Cf. Recital 14 of the Directive 98/44/EC on the Legal Protection of Biotechnological Inventions, OJ EC L 213 of 30 July 1998, p. 13. One may see the possibility to grant licenses as a 'positive' aspect of the rights.

tion.[21] Yet, as an exception, even this 'negative' form of the exercise of a right (preventing competitors from using the protected subject-matter) may be considered as abusive conduct[22] (I will return to that later).

Nevertheless, it must be said that the anti-trust law may be a way of protecting IPRs by enabling the right holder to use them. For example, in the *Intel* case the anti-trust law was applied against the undertaking that held the dominant position in the market and used it in order to prevent the IPRs owner to exercise the rights.[23]

One may now ask the question which is in the focus of this paper: i.e. whether, from the point of view of the anti-trust law, intellectual property needs to be regarded in the same way as tangible property or not. The answer is far from unambiguous. In the *Magill* case the ECJ decided that intellectual property has a special status and could lead to greater restriction of competition[24]. In particular, the court said that the anti-trust law should take precedence only when a rejection of a license prevents the development of a secondary market to the detriment of consumers.[25] Yet in the Microsoft case the Commission and the CFI, regarded IPRs as if they were tangible property such as ports or train tracks.[26]

Considering the influence of IPRs on competition, it is important to take into consideration the dominant position of an IPR holder. Owning of an exclusive right itself does not necessarily mean holding a dominant (or even monopolistic) position in the sense of the anti-trust law.[27] Usually the subject-matter protected by IPRs has substitutes. But even if a legal monopoly is grounded in an economic monopoly, it is not a sufficient reason to demand that the protected matter should be offered to third parties. This is because the exclusive right should encourage investment and making new innovations. Therefore a rejection of a license abuses the anti-trust law only in exceptional circumstances, i.e. if it involves an additional factor (that is, if it includes an additional anti-trust ele-

21 Cf. A. Ch. Beunen (*supra* note 18), p. 236.

22 E.g. ECJ in the *Magill* case.

23 Cf. A. Heinemann, *Compulsory Licenses and Product Integration in European Anti-trust law – Assessment of the European Commission's Microsoft Decision*, 36 IIC 63, 82 (2005), especially note 91 where the author pointed to the *Microsoft* case as an example.

24 This view has been subscribed to Cf. A. Heinemann (*supra* note 23), p. 71.; S. Anderman (*supra* note 12, p. 8) said that in the *Magill* case a proof of a special treatment of IPRs by the ECJ is in the 'exceptional circumstances' test. However, J. Temple Lang (*supra* note 3, p. 4) emphasized that the position holds when it is accepted that the *Magill* conditions determining the rules of compulsory encroachment on the scope of the legal exclusivity are cumulative in nature.

25 A. Heinemann (*supra* note 23), p. 71.

26 Cf. S. Anderman (*supra* note 12), p.18. This opinion is shared by some other authors; cf. A. Heinemann (*supra* note 23), p.71.

27 Cf. e.g. J. Temple Lang (*supra* note 3), p. 18; Bellamy&Child, *European Community Law of Competition*, 2001, p. 710.

ment[28]). A view has been presented that the additional 'active anti-trust conduct' concerns cases when abuse of a dominant position blocks innovative markets[29] because IPRs are often used to reserve for oneself 'normal' markets like, for example, the information access market.[30] Before the legitimacy of any abuse of a dominant position by preventing the third parties from the IP subject-matter use is assessed, it is crucial to determine if for the third party the subject-matter is 'indispensable' to operate[31] (in the sense that there are neither actual nor potential substitutes for it).[32] This is a clear reference to the American 'essential facility doctrine'.[33] Let us focus on this issue now. The principle of access to 'essential facilities' in the USA is a hundred years old,[34] although its existence is sometimes challenged.[35] The phrase 'essential facility' was first used by the Commission in the *Sea Containers v. Stena Sealink* case.[36] Essential facilities are related to the so-called bottleneck problem. It concerns cases in which an undertaking controls the goods whose use is a condition for the operations of another undertaking in a given market, and whose replacement is practically impossible.[37]

'Essential facilities' include raw materials, services, information or access to certain places such as sea ports or airports; they also include IPRs.[38] The dominant undertaking that has actual or legal access to the essential facility uses them but refuses access to competitors (either totally or by consenting to grant access

28 J. Temple Lang (*supra* note 3), p. 18.

29 Net Le, *Intellectual Property Protection for Non-Innovative Markets: The Case of IMS Health,* (2006) Erasmus Law and Economics Review Vol. 2 No. 1, p. 91. The author thinks that in the case of an innovative market abuse can happen only if two markets can be distinguished and the IPR blocks one of them (p. 98).

30 It is difficult to talk of an 'innovative market' for example with regard to blocking access to information (the *Magill* case) or *de facto standard* (the *IMS* case) – a point to be focused on below.

31 The 'indispensability' test is carried out objectively, i.e. the fact that the behaviour of the dominant undertaking negatively affects one particular undertaking is irrelevant. Cf. J. Temple Lang (*supra* note 3), p. 6.

32 Cf. the *Bronner* and *Magill* cases (below).

33 Cf. I. Haracoglou (*supra* note 2), p. 133.

34 Cf. U.S. Supreme Court 224 U.S. 383 (1912) – *US v. Terminal Railroad Association of ST. Louis.*

35 It must be pointed out that in the *Trinko* case (540 US 398 (2004)), the U.S. Supreme Court made a surprising statement that the Court 'never recognized such a doctrine'; cf. J. Viniol (*supra* notes 8 and 1), p. 91, note 33.

36 OJ EC L 15 of 18 January 1994, p. 8. It is characteristic that the term is not used by the ETS; Cf. Advocate General Jacobs in Case C-7/97, ECR 1998, I-7791 – *Bronner v. Mediaprint.*

37 Access to facilities is not essential if competitors can make a (competitive) facility; J. Temple Lang (*supra* note 3), p. 10 f.

38 Advocate General Jacobs in Case C-7/97, ECR 1998, I-7791, 7806-7807 – *Bronner v. Mediaprint.*

on unacceptable terms[39]) without an objective justification.[40] As a result, the competitors are unable to provide services to their customers. This violates the provisions of Art. 102 TFEU (but only if the other terms stipulated in the regulation are fulfilled).[41] In the *Bronner*[42] case the ECJ decided that a *facility is essential if no real or potential alternatives exist*[43]. A typical example is a situation in which there are two markets,[44] that is if an entrepreneur uses his dominant position on market 'A' (the downstream market, such as the market of the only accessible raw material) in order to protect his position on the 'connected' market 'B' (the upstream market, e.g. the market of products made from this raw material). The *Bronner* case, however, concerned only one market, i.e. the press delivery market.[45] It should be emphasized that the very fact of monopolization of a market by allowable means and the consequent attainment of competitive advantage cannot be regarded as a case of blocking access to an essential facility. Abuse of dominant position happens only when a dominant player owning the IPRs uses them in order to gain leverage or to protect oneself from competition in another, distinct market[46]. As a result, competition is eliminated[47] or at least all effective competition is eliminated.[48] The idea of essential facilities in practice means that, by definition, the holder of an essential facility holds the domi-

39 This regards primarily the excessively high process (cf. the *Volvo and Renault* case). By way of comparison it must be said that under the American Sherman Act excessive pricing would not constitute an illegal practice; cf. J. Temple Lang (*supra* note 3), p. 22.

40 Having an IPR is not in itself an 'objective justification'; CFI in the *Microsoft* case - September 2007. Also see I. Haracoglou (*supra* note 2), p. 139. The reasons enumerated in the decisions that justified the barring from essential facilities were pointed out by J. Temple Lang (*supra* note 3), p. 22 et seq.

41 Cf. Commission Decision, OJ EC L 15 of 18 January 1994, p. 8 – *Sea Containers – Stena Sealink.*

42 ECR 1998, I-7791.

43 According to the ECJ, in order for the condition of the lack of 'potential alternative' to be met it must be at least shown that undertaking production on a scale comparable to that of the controlling undertaking the 'essential facility' is not economically viable.

44 The requirement of two markets is not, however, obvious in the light of the *IMS* case discussed below.

45 A newspaper publisher *Bronner* refused the competitor use of its home delivery service. Although the ECJ did not see in this particular case any abuse of the rules of competition but, at the same time, indicated 'exceptional circumstances' in which such rules would be violated. Let me underline that, chronologically speaking, the *Bronner* case has changed the rules determined in the *Magill* case discussed below, but since the decision did not concern IPRs I have presented them here.

46 J. Temple Lang (*supra* note 3), pp. 12 and 19.

47 Cf. especially the *Commercial Solvents* (1974) and *Bronner* (1998) cases.

48 The *Microsoft* case, para. 563.

nant position on every market that requires access to the facility. As a consequence, there is no need to determine the relevant market.[49]

The problem of abuse of a dominant position resulting from the exercise of IPRs was taken into consideration by the Commission in its "Guidance on the Commission's enforcement priorities in applying Art. 82 of the EC Treaty to abusive exclusionary conduct by dominant undertakings".[50]

In particular, it was reasoned that refusal to supply, illegal under Art. 102 of TFEU, is a concept that covers a broad range of practices, such as refusal to supply products to existing or new customers,[51] refusal to licence intellectual property rights,[52] including situations when the license is necessary to provide interface information,[53] or refusal to grant access to an essential facility or a network (para. 78).

The Commission does not regard it as necessary for the refused product to have been already traded: it is sufficient that there is demand from potential purchasers and that a potential market for the input at stake can be identified.[54] Likewise, it is not necessary for there to be actual refusal on the part of a dominant undertaking; "constructive refusal" is sufficient. Constructive refusal could, for example, take the form of unduly delaying or otherwise degrading the supply of the product or involve the imposition of unreasonable conditions in return for the supply (para. 79).

Finally, instead of refusing to supply, a dominant undertaking may charge a price for the product on the upstream market which, compared to the price it charges on the downstream market,[55] does not allow even an equally efficient competitor to trade profitably in the downstream market on a lasting basis (a so-called 'margin squeeze'). In margin-squeeze cases the benchmark which the Commission will generally rely on to determine the costs of an equally efficient

49 Cf. *Commission guidelines on market analysis and the assessment of significant market power under the Community regulatory framework for electronic communications networks and services*, OJ EC C 165 of 11 July 2002, p. 6, para. 81.

50 Commission document C(2009) 864 final of 9 February 2009.

51 ECJ, joined Cases 6/73 and 7/73, ECR 1974, 223 – *Istituto Chemioterapico Italiano and Commercial Solvents v. Commission.*

52 ECJ, joined Cases C-241/91 P and C-242/91 P, ECR 1995, 743 – *Radio Telefis Eireann (RTE) and Independent Television Publications Ltd (ITP) v. Commission (Magill)*; Case C-418/01, ECR 2004, I-5039 – *IMS Health v. NDC Health.* Those judgments show that in exceptional circumstances a refusal to license intellectual property rights is abusive.

53 See CFI, Case T-201/04, ECR 2007, II-3601 – *Microsoft v. Commission.*

54 Case C-418/01, ECR 2004, I-5039, para. 44 – *IMS Health v. NDC Health.*

55 Including a situation in which an integrated undertaking that sells a "system" of complementary products refuses to sell one of the complementary products on an unbundled basis to a competitor that produces the other complementary product.

competitor are the long-run average incremental cost of the downstream division of the integrated dominant undertaking[56] (para. 80).

The Commission will consider these practices as an enforcement priority if all the following circumstances are present:

- the refusal relates to a product or service that is objectively necessary to be able to compete effectively on a downstream market,
- the refusal is likely to lead to the elimination of effective competition on the downstream market, and
- the refusal is likely to lead to consumer harm (para. 81).

In certain specific cases, it may be clear that imposing an obligation to supply is manifestly not capable of having negative effects on the input owner's and/or other operators' incentives to invest and innovate upstream, whether ex ante or ex post. The Commission considers that this is particularly likely to be the case where regulation compatible with Community law already imposes an obligation to supply on the dominant undertaking and it is clear, from the considerations underlying such a regulation, that the necessary balancing of incentives has already been made by the public authority when imposing such an obligation to supply. This could also be the case where the upstream market position of the dominant undertaking has been developed under the protection of special or exclusive rights or has been financed by state resources. In such specific cases there is no reason for the Commission to deviate from its general enforcement standard of showing likely anti-trust foreclosure, without considering whether the three circumstances referred to in paragraph 81 are present (para. 82).

In the Guidance, the Commission has also offered an explanation of the circumstances enumerated in paragraph 81 (83-89) and the concept of benefits in the form of an efficiency gains, which often happens to be the dominant undertaking's argument (whose purpose is to show that the means used by the undertaking do not abuse the market position (89-90).

The Commission's stand is quite general and does not go beyond its previous practice and the ECJ decisions.

To close the introductory part of this paper I'd like to draw attention to the necessity to distinguish between compulsory licenses in the meaning of the provisions protecting industrial property and access to IPRs on the basis of the anti-trust law. In the former case the conditions, including the royalty rate, are determined by the license granting body (usually the patent office), whereas in the latter case the body protecting competition ascertains anti-trust behaviour, requiring

56 In some cases, however, the LRAIC of a non-integrated competitor downstream might be used as the benchmark, for example when it is not possible to clearly allocate the dominant undertaking's costs to downstream and upstream operations.

that it be discontinued. The exclusive right holder is thus imposed a duty to deal[57] and the terms of the contract are defined by an agreement between the same parties.[58] It is also important that compulsory licenses that IP protecting regulations provide for are granted *ex ante*, while the licenses provided for by the anti-trust law are granted *ex post.*[59]

2. Copyright

2.1 Legal standing

Copyright law does not provide for the grant of compulsory licenses. This does not mean that third persons may use works only with the consent of the right holder since the limitations of copyright are allowed in a relatively broad scope. An important relevant regulation is to be found in Art. 6 of the EC Computer Program Directive, which permits decompilation of a program thus enabling its interoperability.[60] At the same time Recital 26 of the Directive states that the provisions of the Directive are without prejudice to the application of the competition rules under Art. 85 EC (now 101 TFEU) and 86 EC (now 102 TFEU) if the dominant supplier refuses to make available information which is necessary for interoperability as defined in that directive.

2.2 Court decisions

Precedential decisions were issued in the *Magill, Ladbroke, IMS* and *Microsoft* cases. There was also an interesting decision issued in Poland with regard to the Polish Collecting Society ZAiKS.

57 Cf. I. Haracoglou (*supra* note 2), p. 122. As highlighted by other authors, *one of the most spectacular phenomena in market economy is the restriction of contractual freedom by imposing an obligation to contract;* cf. A. Heinemann (*supra* note 23), p. 63. Of course the obligation-to-contract situation is a broader concept than the compulsory-license case, as it is not limited to an infringement of the scope of IPRs; cf. A. Heinemann (*supra* note 23), p. 69.

58 In certain circumstances it may happen that an agreement resulting from a duty to deal imposed on the dominant undertaking as such will abuse the anti-monopoly law, in particular if it is an exclusive license preventing other undertakings from access to the essential facility.

59 A. Ch. Beunen (*supra* note 18), p. 260.

60 S. Anderman (*supra* note 12), p.18.

(a) *Magill* case (1995)[61]: Magill Company intended to publish a weekly TV guide covering all stations. In the UK television guides are copyrighted works. Two stations refused to grant licenses to publish their TV program listings. In this case, for the first time, the ECJ decided that in exceptional cases it is possible to grant a compulsory license based on the anti-trust law.[62]

According to the ECJ, copyright cannot prevent competitors from publishing the TV listings and the refusal to grant a license is, in view of the circumstances, an abuse of a dominant position. In the said case the court recognized the following exceptional circumstances:

There was no actual or potential substitute for the TV guide that would list all programs. The refusal to grant a license caused an absence of a new product on the market where there was a potential demand for it.

There was no justification for such a refusal, and by their action the broadcasters reserved for themselves the secondary market of weekly TV guides by excluding all competition on that market.

It was highlighted in the doctrine that the significance of the decision depends on whether the conditions indicated in paragraph 1 (preventing a new product from appearing on the market) and paragraph 3 (appropriation of the secondary market resulting the fact that IPRs are an 'essential imput'[63]) must be met cumulatively or not.[64]

It must be emphasized, however, that the case circumstances were unusual and its relation with IPRs was merely a result of a special understanding of the copyright subject-matter in the UK. It was, as a matter of fact, a problem of access to information with no creative element. A TV guide itself is a kind of database.[65]

(b) *Ladbroke* case (1997)[66]: The copyright holders of French horse racing refused to grant Ladbroke a license to show the races in Belgian betting shops. The CFI decided that the duty to deal had not arisen as the subject-matter of copyright was neither essential to Ladbroke operations nor prevented a new product from being launched onto the market.[67] Apparently the CFI was in favour of a broad interpretation of the position taken in the *Magill* case, recognizing that the

61 ECR 1995, I-743.

62 Cf. J. Temple Lang (*supra* note 3): As to the nature of the forbidden practice the ECJ assumed that depriving viewers of one (joined) TV guide and make them buy a publication of each broadcaster had (also) the character of an exploitive practice, p. 22.

63 I. Haracoglou (*supra* note 2), p. 160.

64 Cf. J. Viniol (*supra* note 16), p. 90.

65 Cf. A.Ch. Beunen (*supra* note 18), p. 237 f.

66 ECR 1997, I-6265.

67 Cf. J.Temple Lang (*supra* note 3), p.17.

requirements in respect of the new product role and the leverage rule were separate.[68]

(c) *IMS Health* case (2004)[69]: *IMS* is a company that collects pharmaceutical data, operating in more than 100 countries. Among other things, it collects pharmaceuticals sales statistics, based on its own system of a country division into 1860 parts called the 'brick structure', copyrighted in Germany, from which the data is obtained. The division is a 'common language' for companies analyzing sales trends.[70] It is the information coming from the brick-structure system that is used by undertakings to support their marketing strategies. The brick structure is a *de facto* standard.[71] Basing on copyright of reproduction, *IMS* effectively prevented competition from using the 'brick structure'; it also refused to grant licenses. As a result, an alternative system could not be created. One of the competitors instituted proceedings, accusing IMS of abusing the dominant position.[72]

The Commission (and later the ECJ) primarily concluded that a compulsory encroachment on IPRs may take place as long as these rights prevent access to products or services essential for carrying on a particular business. This is a clear reference to the essential-facility doctrine adopted in the above-mentioned *Bronner case*[73]. In the case discussed it was decided that the 1860 bricks structure was indispensable to operating a business on the relevant market as there was no actual or potential substitute for it.[74] Speaking more generally, the *de facto standard* was seen as an essential facility.[75]

If a refusal to grant a license concerns an indispensable copyrighted material then the dominant position is being abused if the following conditions are jointly met:

- the IPR owner prevents in this way a competitive product or service from appearing on the market while there is potential demand for it,[76]

68 I. Haracoglou (*supra* note 2), p. 162; The author emphasizes the crucial role of a market definition when deciding if an IPR holder has abused a dominant position by refusing to licence a product.

69 Case C-418/01, ECR 2004, I-5039 – *IMS Health v. NDC Health.*

70 Cf. D. W. Hull, J. R. Atwood, J. B. Perrine, *Compulsory Licensing*, The European Antitrust Review 2002, p. 36.

71 Cf. np. I. Haracoglou (*supra* note 2), p. 166.

72 Cf. D. W. Hull, J. R. Atwood, J. B. Perrine (*supra* note 70), p. 36.

73 A. Heinemann (*supra* note 23), p. 70.

74 Cf. D. W. Hull, J. R. Atwood, J. B. Perrine (*supra* note 70), p. 36.

75 Cf. A. Ch. Beunen (*supra* note 18), p. 240, note 33.

76 It is said in the doctrine that a 'new' product is considered i.e. one that was referred to in the *Magill case*. A. Heinemann (*supra* note 23), p. 71; the author says that it is in reference to this that condition that there is a significant difference between tangible property and 'normal' essential facility case. In 'normal' cases the European anti-trust law prohibits in a general way the use of economic power to conquer neighbouring markets if suc-

- there is no objective justification for the refusal,
- the refusal to grant a license leads to a reservation of a market for the supply of information on the sales of pharmaceutical products, resulting in a total elimination of competition.

It is said in the doctrine that in the *IMS* case the *Magill* conditions were cumulatively applied.[77] In fact the conditions in the two cases are markedly different. First, the fact of data transfer based on the brick structure creates a situation where there is literally no case when the emergence of a truly novel (i.e. previously unknown) product was prevented. What is meant then is a failure to admit a competing business that offers the same product (information on the sales of pharmaceutical products). Second, in the *Magill* case two markets were identified (of which the downstream market was not occupied). Yet, as a consequence of the decision issued in the *IMS* case, a real competitor was admitted to the market since there had already been an IPR owner on that market. Therefore the admittance of a competitor adversely affected the core interest of the IP owner.[78]

The doubts raised with respect to this case are analogous to those in the *Magill* case: should the brick structure have been considered as a work in the meaning of copyright? The case was really about access to a *de facto standard*, indispensable for creating a database of medicinal products. In case of lack of copyright protection, using a common standard in creating one's own database would be basically permitted.

(d) *Microsoft* case (2007)[79]: Microsoft infringed Art. 102 by abusing its dominant position in two ways: 1) by refusal to supply its competitors with interoperability information and by refusal to authorize them to use the information; 2) by making available to customers Windows Operating System on condition they also purchase Windows Media Player.[80] It must be said that the domination of Windows and significant entry barriers were caused by a network effect (caused, on one hand, by the number of users and, on the other hand, by the number of applications written for Windows). The network effect leads to a natural monop-

cess on these markets is not due to competition on the merits (*ibidem* p. 71). In fact no 'new' product appeared in the *IMS* case. This is discussed later.

77 A. Heinemann (*supra* note 23), p. 70.

78 Cf. Net Le (*supra* note 29), p. 95. The author says that IPRs protected a crucial component of the market (p. 96 et seq.).

79 ECR 2007, II-3601.

80 Cf. P.-A. Dubois, Sh. Yavorsky, *The Microsoft decision: the evolution of compulsory licensing in the European Union*, in: IP Value 2008: *Building and enforcing intellectual property value*, p. 119 f.

oly.[81] The domination of Windows was established in such a way that the system could be described as a *de facto* standard.[82]

With respect to the first issue, the Court of First Instance (CFI) sustained the Commission's decision,[83] assuming that, although an entrepreneur may, in general, make his own choice of business partners, in exceptional circumstances a refusal to supply from a dominant undertaking may be an abuse of that position. It is pointed out in literature that, in contrast to the *Magill* case, the 'exceptional circumstances' test was radically changed by a considerable extension of its scope. Namely, the Commission (and the CFI) followed the path indicated by the Commercial Solvents (and subsequent decisions[84]), assuming that if the dominant undertaking that owns a no-substitute product and maintains business contacts with a contractor operating on the aftermarket suddenly decides on a vertical integration and launching one's own product on that market, it may be obliged to continue supplies (in this case to grant a license or make information available) to former contractors (who are now competing on that market) unless it is capable of offering an objective justification of the refusal to supply. Thus, in the light of the decision in the *Magill* case, such an obligation may also be applied, under Art. 102 TFEU, to IP-protected products.[85] Since the Microsoft's competitor also offered an innovative product (and not just a 'clone' of the Microsoft product), it was justified to accuse Microsoft of actions whose aim was the 'technological leveraging of its dominance'.[86]

The CFI applied a three-step test to prove an abuse of a dominant position: First, the refusal of access must concern a product or a service which is indispensable to exercise activity on a neighbouring market. The fact that the indispensible product or service is not introduced into circulation separately from the product or service with regard to which the undertaking holds the dominant position does not affect the possibility to identify two different markets.

Second, the refusal must prevent any effective competition on a given market. The very risk of competition elimination is sufficient; it is not necessary to show that all competitors active on a market will be eliminated.

Third, the refusal must cause non-emergence on the market of a new product for which there exists customer demand.

81 Cf. A. Heinemann (*supra* note 23), pp. 67 (and note 19) and 82.

82 Cf. A. Heinemann (*supra* note 23), p. 67.

83 CFI of 17 September 2007, Case T-201/04, ECR 2007, II-3601 – *Microsoft Corp. v. Comission of the European Communities.*

84 E.g. Case 311/84, ECR 1985, 3261 – *CBEM v. Telemarketing.*

85 Cf. S. Anderman (*supra* note 12), p. 7.

86 Cf. S. Anderman (*supra* note 12), p. 15 and note 40.

As shown in the literature, it is questionable if in the Microsoft case the possibility of introducing a new product that was not offered by Microsoft was indeed prevented.[87]

Besides, in the matter discussed the Commission concluded that the anti-trust law applied automatically, regardless of the right to decompilation provided for in the already mentioned Art. 6 of the EC Computer Program Directive.

It was rightly stated in the doctrine, however, that if IP law offered a broader scope of interoperability of interface information for software, Art. 82 (now 102 TFEU) would be applied even less frequently in the event of non-supply of interface information.[88]

As for the second issue (the bundling of the Windows PC operating system and Windows Media Player), the CFI also accepted the position of the Commission by concluding that the dominant position had been abused because

1) the undertaking held the dominant position;
2) the tying product and the tied product were separate,
3) the consumer did not have a choice of purchasing only one product,
4) the practice must have resulted in foreclosure of competition.[89]

It ought to be underlined that in the Microsoft case the Commission went further than the US competition authorities which came in for even official criticism.[90]

As can be seen the criteria for the abuse of a dominant position have considerably differed from those in the cases discussed so far.

In the subsequent proceedings against Microsoft, on 15 January 2009 the Commission issued the Statement of Objections on the tying of the Internet Explorer to Windows.[91] However, no substantive proceedings took place because Microsoft prepared a document called 'Commitment' in which it promised to give the European users of Windows the possibility to choose other Internet browsers, and offer both the hardware producers and users the possibility to switch the Internet Explorer off. Microsoft also promised to publish a statement in which in-depth information would be disclosed so that interoperability of other products with the Windows OS would be facilitated.[92] On 16 December

87 So it stands to question whether the requirement defined in the *Magill case* was in this respect fulfilled. Cf. A. Heinemann (*supra* note 23), p. 72.

88 S. Anderman (*supra* note 12), p. 19.

89 Cf. Cf. P.-A. Dubois, Sh. Yavorsky (*supra* note 80), p. 120.

90 H. Pate, head of antitrust division of the DoJ concluded that *it is unfortunate that the largest fine ever was imposed in a case of unilateral conduct, the most ambiguous and controversial area of antitrust enforcement* (after A. Heinemann (*supra* note 23, p. 65, note 5).

91 Case COMP/C-3/39.530 – *Microsoft* (tying).

92 See Proposed Commitment of 6 October 2009 and 'Commitment' of 1 December 2009.

2009 the Commission issued a decision (based on Art. 9 of Regulation 1/2003[93]) which had a binding effect on the Microsoft's commitments.[94]

Also in Poland the President of the Polish Office of Competition and Consumer Protection (OCCP) conducted explanatory proceedings in December 2007 in order to initially establish whether there was an unlawful agreement between Microsoft and notebook manufacturers restricting competition whereby the manufacturers were obliged to sell only notebooks with the pre-installed Windows operating system. Since the consequences of the agreement could affect the whole territory of the EU the collected materials were handed over to the Commission.[95]

(e) *ZAiKS* case (1995)[96]: A case was heard in Poland that concerned an accusation by the RMF radio station that the Polish Collecting Society ZAiKS abused the dominant position with regard to the radio broadcaster RMF. RMF was obliged to pay 6 per cent from its advertising revenues for copyright use. Besides the commercial advertisements proper, RMF also derived income from paid announcements. The conflict arose around the interpretation of the phrase 'advertising revenues', namely whether the 6 per cent payment to ZAiKS was to be based solely on the commercial advertising proper or also on the paid announcements. ZAiKS, which unsurprisingly was in favour of the broad interpretation of the phrase 'advertising revenues', disaffirmed the agreement, to which RMF responded by getting the case before the President of the Polish Office of Competition and Consumer Protection (OCCP).

The OCCP President concluded that even if ZAiKS had been right, it should have pursued a claim in the court to examine the content of the agreement. He considered the failure to prosecute the claim and the sole disaffirmation of the agreement as an abuse of a dominant position (in view of the fact that RMF had no other access to the works without which it could not carry on its activities) and ordered to cease the practice.[97] The decision was overruled by the Polish Court for Consumer and Competition Protection but accepted the OCCP President's judgement as to the principle.[98]

93 In case the duties are not fulfilled, the Commission can impose a fine without having to prove that community competition rules have been violated.

94 Commission Decision of 16 December 2009 relating to proceedings under Art. 102 of TFEU (Case COMP/C-3/39.530 – *Microsoft* (tying).

95 Cf. Ł. Gorywoda, A. Jańczuk, *UOKiK v. Microsoft: stosowanie prawa konkurencji w sektorach nowej gospodarki a ryzyko błędu regulacyjnego*, PSEAP Working Paper No. 3/2009, p. 2 et seqq.

96 "Wokanda" 1997, No. 2, p. 47.

97 Decision DO-II-57/S/2/94/591 (indicated in the verdict quoted below of 20 December 1995).

98 Verdict of 20 December 1995, XVII Amr 49/95; „Orzecznictwo Sądu Antymonopolowego" 1997, No. 3, p. 47 et seqq.

2.3 Conclusion

The final decision depended on the particular state of affairs. In two cases (*Magill* and *IMS*) the decision to grant a compulsory license followed a very questionable assumption that copyright had been abused. In the *Microsoft* case the exceptional circumstance was due to the network effect. It would be difficult to make conclusions as to the future decisions; they will be affected mostly by particular 'circumstances' that the Commission and the ECJ consider as 'exceptional'.

3. Inventions

"The tension between patent and anti-trust law erupted at most from the inception of anti-trust law in the late 19-th and early 20-th century. In the 1930s and 40s, the US Supreme Court rejected isolation of patents from anti-trust law. In an inspired attempt to reconcile the two bodies of law, the Court reasoned that anti-trust law is free to operate when patent holders reach beyond the boundaries inherent in the patent grant."[99]

3.1 Legal standing

Following the Doha Declaration[100] the TRIPS agreement was amended. Namely Paragraph 6 of the Doha Declaration provided for the situation where pharmaceutical products protected by copyright in a developing country are indispensable to facilitate public health care and, as a consequence, there is basis to grant a compulsory license. However, due to lack of sufficient production capacities in such a country, it is not possible to make such products there. Under Art. 31bis TRIPS products can be actually made in another country. In this situation a patent infringement proceeding against an actual manufacturer of a pharmaceutical cannot be launched.[101] The European Union issued Regulation (EC) No. 816/2006 of 17 May 2006 on compulsory licensing of patents relating to the manufacture of pharmaceutical products for export to countries with public

99 R. Feldman, *Patent and Antitrust: Differing Shades of Meaning*, 13 Virginia Journal of Law and Technology 3, 5 (2008); see also the decisions mentioned in note 13.

100 World Trade Organization; document WT/MIN(01)/DEC/2, 20 November 2001.

101 M. du Vall, *Prawo patentowe*, p. 114 et seq. (Warszawa 2008).

health problems[102] thus establishing an approval procedure to enable export of patent-protected products to developing countries.

The Proposal for a Council Regulation on the Community patent of 2000[103] also needs to be mentioned. Art. 21(3) of that proposal empowered the Commission to authorise the exploitation of a patent in some specific situations. These are times of crisis, extreme emergencies or situations where it is necessary to remedy a practice determined after judicial or administrative process to be anti-trust.

Rules that envisage abuse of anti-trust law as a basis for grant of compulsory licenses can also be found in national legislations. For example, under the provisions of a repealed Polish law of 1972 on inventive activity[104] a possible anti-trust violation case was indicated of employing monopolistic practices as one of the ways to misuse a patent that served as basis for granting a compulsory patent in a proceeding before the Patent Office.[105]

By contrast in the American Patent Act of 1988 it was indicated that, if the patent holder has market power, then his tying of license grant with the demand to purchase a separate product may be considered as patent misuse.[106] Also in the Australian *Intellectual Property Laws Amendment Act 2006* a compulsory license grant was envisaged on grounds of anti-trust conduct by the right holder violating provisions of the *Trade Practice Act 1974*.[107]

102 OJ EC L 157 of 9 June 2006, p. 1.

103 In the Proposal for Council Regulation on the Community patent, COM(2000) 412 final of 1 August 2000.

104 "Dziennik Ustaw" (Journal of Laws of the Republic of Poland) 1984, No. 33, para. 177.

105 This raised doubts as to whether the assessment could be made by the Patent Office alone or whether a prior decision by the President of the Polish Office of Competition and Consumer Protection was necessary. In the Act on industrial property rights the independence of the two proceedings was directly stated. Under para. 4 of Art. 68 of the Polish Industrial Property Law of 2000, the cite provisions concerning abuse of law do not violated the provisions concerning anti-trust practices.

106 35 U.S.C. § 271(d)(5) (2000); Cf. R. Feldman (*supra* note 99), p. 7. It should be added that under the Public Health Emergencies Act US Secretary of Health and Human Services has broad discretion to issue compulsory licenses to address public health emergencies. Using this as a basis, in 2001 the Secretary of HHS applied for a compulsory license to use a Bayer's pharmaceutical, which couldn't be supplied by the firm in sufficient amount; Cf. I. Haracoglou (*supra* note 2), p. 62 and notes 110-113.

107 K. Gibbson, Z. Fazal, *Anti-competitive conduct could result in a compulsory licence*, 2007, available at http://www.freehills.com.au/2078.aspx.

3.2 Court decisions

(a) *GlaxoSmithKline* case (2008)[108]: Glaxo declined to carry out an order placed by Greek wholesalers who exported the purchased goods to other member states. The ECJ concluded that abuse of a dominant position does not take place if the refusal [...] to supply wholesalers involved in parallel exports constitutes a reasonable and proportionate measure in relation to the threat that those exports represent to its legitimate commercial interests [...] (para. 70). In particular, the Advocate-General was of an opinion that the refusal to supply wholesalers with the intention of restraining parallel trade might be justified in pharmaceutical industry mostly relating to the high level of regulation and sunk cost of R&D.[109] Should a dominant pharmaceutical company, however, refuse to meet 'ordinary' orders from a wholesaler, it is abusing its dominant position (para. 77).[110]

The important factors determining the fulfilment of the 'ordinary orders' condition are the size of the orders in relation to the size of the member state's market and the previous business relations with the particular wholesaler.[111]

The number of cases that are examined in EC member states relating to the compulsory license problem under the anti-trust law is small. At the same time, the decisions are completely different.

(b) Let us look at the *Intel Corporation v. Via Technologies Inc.* case[112] examined in Britain. *Intel* had patents protecting computer hardware. Via obtained a license to make chipsets for several processors but not the newest Pentium 4. *Via* started producing chipsets which were compatible with the new processor. Intel held patents covering the interconnection between the Pentium 4 and the associated chipset and brought a patent infringement action in the UK since *Via* chipsets had to use the patented interconnect technology. *Via* in particular said that Art. 82 EC (now Art. 102 TFEU) was violated. In its 'Euro-defence' *Via* raised an argument that the patent-protected interconnect technology was a *de facto* industrial standard.

108 Joined Cases C-468/06 to C-478/06 – *Sot. Lélos kai Sia EE and Others v. GlaxoSmith Kline AEVE Farmakeftikon Proionton, formerly Glaxowellcome AEVE*, available at: http://eur-lex.europa.eu/LexUriServ/LexUriServ.do?uri=CELEX:62006J0468:EN:HTML. Note that the Competition Commission in the Republic of South Africa concluded that the same company violated anti-trust law of that country by an abuse of a dominant position in the anti-retroviral markets by virtue of excessive pricing; cf. I. Haracoglou (*supra* note 2), p. 63, note 114.

109 I. Haracoglou (*supra* note 2), p. 170.

110 Joined Cases C-468/06 to C-478/06 – *Sot. Lélos kai Sia EE and Others v. GlaxoSmith-Kline AEVE Farmakeftikon Proionton, formerly Glaxowellcome AEVE* (*supra* note 108).

111 Joined Cases C-468/06 to C-478/06 – *Sot. Lélos kai Sia EE and Others v. GlaxoSmith-Kline AEVE Farmakeftikon Proionton, formerly Glaxowellcome AEVE* (*supra* note 108).

112 Cf. A. Tautoungi, *Holding Back the Tide of Compulsory Licensing?*, 2002 EIPR 548.

The British court reasoned that the national patent systems had their inherent instruments to ensure the balance of interests of the right holders and the third parties by enabling to grant compulsory licenses in the public interest, and by their temporary character. With respect to the Community case law the court concluded that it concerned copyright and with respect to patents it cannot be assumed that a refusal to grant a license is inadmissible because it leads to the elimination of competition. An opposite stand would completely undermine the purpose of patent protection.[113]

(c) In Italy the Competition Authority decided that refusal to grant a patent license may signify an abuse of a dominant position. In the case examined, Merck refused to grant Dobfar a license for an active ingredient needed to produce particular medicines. Strictly speaking, the protection was not under a patent (since it had expired) but under the Supplementary Protection Certificate, a fact which does not affect the essence of the problem. However, it must be brought to attention that the justification of the decision raised many questions, in particular because it was assumed that manufacturing patented medicines in Italy did not infringe the exclusive rights granted in that country if the production is for the export to countries where the patent had expired.[114]

(d) *Orange Book Standard* case (2009): The German Supreme Court issued a significant decision concerning 'anti-trust law defence' in patent infringement cases.[115] Philips protected Compact Disc by patents. The protected inventions that were the subject of the disagreement had become a standard (the *Orange Book Standard*). Philips readily granted licenses to many undertakings. The defendant, however, started production without obtaining a license, claiming that the royalties demanded by Philips were excessive and discriminating. Although in the examined case the court concluded that the patent had indeed been infringed as the entrepreneur had not applied for a license before applying the invention, it indicated principles on which it would be acceptable to efficiently invoke the abuse of a dominant position in patent infringement litigations. They are as follows:

a) the patent owner holds the dominant position since no alternative technology exists,

b) the defendant offered to sign a licensing agreement on appropriate terms,

113 A. Tautoungi (*supra* note 112), p. 551. The judge stressed that in the published Decisions USA there are no known cases of compulsory license grants on grounds of unilateral refusal to grant a patent license (cf. *Image Technical Services* note 18.)

114 R. Coco, P. Nebbia, *Compulsory licencing and interim measures in Merck: a case for Italy of for antitrust law*? (2007) 2 (7) Journal of Intellectual Property Law & Practice 453.

115 German Federal Court of Justice (BGH) of 6 May 2009, Case KZR 39/06, 2009 GRUR 694 = 41 IIC 369 (2010) - *Orange-Book-Standard.*

c) the said offer was turned down by the right holder,
d) the rejection of the offer was not backed by an objective justification.[116]

3.3 Conclusion

The possibility to grant a compulsory license under the anti-trust law in the case of patented inventions is usually irrelevant because compulsory licenses, which in particular situations enable encroachment on the exclusive rights of the right holder, are built into the patent law system. Hence it seems to be proper to defend the position of the British court which considered the grant of compulsory licenses under the anti-trust law as inadmissible.

4. Designs

4.1 Legal standing

Art. 26(1) TRIPS provides that 'the owner of a protected industrial design shall have the right to prevent third parties not having the owner's consent from making, selling or importing articles bearing or embodying a design which is a copy, or substantially a copy, of the protected design, when such acts are undertaken for commercial purposes.' Member States may provide limited exceptions to the protection of industrial designs, provided that such exceptions do not unreasonably conflict with the normal exploitation of protected industrial designs and do not unreasonably prejudice the legitimate interests of the owner of the protected design, taking account of the legitimate interests of third parties. (para. 2).

Both Directive 98/71/EC of the European Parliament and of the Council of 13 October 1998 on the legal protection of designs and Council Regulation (EC) No. 6/2002 of 12 December 2001 on Community design contain exceptions stated in the quoted TRIPS provisions.

Particular problems emerged in the EU with regard to the restricted possibility of carrying out car repairs due to the protection of car body parts as industrial designs. Namely, in some countries protection of such designs was restricted insofar as making products based on designs and using them in car repairs in order to give it its original look did not infringe exclusive rights, in others the exclu-

116 J. Witting, *German Federal Supreme Court decides in landmark case on competition law defence*, Bird & Bird Electronics Update bulletin. Autumn 2009, p. 3. In conclusion the author expresses doubt, inter alia, as to the compliance of these terms with Art. 82 EC (now Art. 102 TFEU).

sive rights were respected on general terms. The European lawmaker was in favour of the liberalization of spare parts market which found expression in both normative acts. Thus in Recital 19 of the Directive it is stated that the rapid adoption of this Directive has become a matter of urgency for a number of industrial sectors; full-scale approximation of the laws of the Member States on the use of protected designs for the purpose of permitting the repair of a complex product so as to restore its original appearance, where the product incorporating the design or to which the design is applied constitutes a component part of a complex product upon whose appearance the protected design is dependent, cannot be introduced at the present stage; the lack of full-scale approximation of the laws of the Member States on the use of protected designs for such repair of a complex product should not constitute an obstacle to the approximation of those other national provisions of design law which most directly affect the functioning of the internal market; for this reason Member States should in the meantime maintain in force any provisions in conformity with the Treaty relating to the use of the design of a component part used for the purpose of the repair of a complex product so as to restore its original appearance, or, if they introduce any new provisions relating to such use, the purpose of these provisions should be only to liberalise the market in such parts; those Member States which, on the date of entry into force of this Directive, do not provide for protection for designs of component parts are not required to introduce registration of designs for such parts.

The Polish law is an example of the changing law exactly in the direction following the directive towards spare parts market liberalization. In the original Industrial property law of 2000 the protection of the discussed category of designs was not restricted. However, later the law changed. According to Art. 106^1 of the act protection under registered-design law does not apply to a product which is a component part of a complex product for the purpose of the repair of that product so as to restore its original appearance (para. 1). Third persons may use the product that paragraph 1 refers to by manufacturing, offering, introducing into circulation, importing, exporting or using the product incorporating the design, or by storing such a product for the said purposes (para. 2).

Also Regulation (EC) No. 6/2002 on Community designs[117] has restrained in this respect the protection arising from the registration of the design. Under Art. 110(1) protection of a Community design 'shall not exist for a design which constitutes a component part of a complex product used for the purpose of the repair of that complex product so as to restore its original appearance.'

117 Council Regulation (EC) No. 6/2002 of 12 December 2001 on Community designs, *OJ EC L 3 of 5 January 2002, p. 1.*

4.2 Court decisions

With respect to the relations between the protection of utility models and the conditions of competition, the key decisions were issued in the *Volvo* and *Renault* cases[118]. In these litigations car manufacturers protected the appearance of the car body parts as industrial models. They refused to grant licenses to undertakings which intended to produce these parts and use them as spare parts. Those undertakings decided that the refusal was an abuse of a dominant position. In the cases examined the accusation of an abuse of a dominant position was not confirmed but criteria were enumerated for the identification of such abuses. The ECJ concluded that the refusal on the part of the design right owner to grant a license may be abuse of a dominant position if

- the entrepreneur refused to supply spare parts to independent workshops,
- the prices for the spare parts have been set at an 'unfair level' or
- a decision was made to stop manufacturing the spare parts (even though the particular makes of a car were still in use).[119]

In the context of the above provisions Directive 98/71/EC and Council Regulation (EC) No. 6/2002 a note must be made that abuse of a dominant position can be ascertained only with regard to those member states where laws liberalising the spare parts market have not been introduced yet.

4.3 Conclusion

It is, in principle, unnecessary to grant compulsory licenses under the anti-trust law if the domestic designs law has instruments that prevent abuse of exclusive rights, particularly the repairs clause.

5. Trade marks

5.1 Legal standing

In the light of the already quoted Art. 21 TRIPS it would seem that the prohibition to grant compulsory licenses for trade marks is absolute, i.e. its application

118 Case 238/87, ECR 1988, I-6211 – *Volvo v. Veng*; ECR 1988, 6039 – *Cicra et Maxicar v. Renault*.

119 Cf. P.-A. Dubois, Sh. Yavorsky (*supra* note 80), p.121.

extends to anti-trust behaviour (covered in the cited Art. 40(2) TRIPS).[120] In practice it is not.

5.2 Court decisions

There are two kinds of cases where use of trade marks by third parties against the will of the right holder was permitted (and in cases not provided for by the trade mark law). The first is a unique case of the 'Grüne Punkt' (Green Dot) mark; the second covers a whole range of cases concerning re-packaging of medicinal products involving damage to the trade marks placed on the products.

(a) *The Green Dot* case (2009)[121]: In 1992 the German company Der Grüne Punkt – Duales System Deutschland (DSD) started providing collection and recycling service to manufacturers in Germany. DSD registered the "Green Dot" logo as a trade mark. Manufacturers using the DSD system obtained a license to use the Green Dot trade mark. The actual collection of recycling materials was carried out by undertakings which had signed agreements with DSD. The recycling materials collectors were obliged to use the logo.[122] In 2001 the Commission issued two decisions stating that some aspects of the system operations were non-compliant with the rules of competition. In 2007 both decisions were upheld by the CFI.[123]

In the first case the Commission concluded that charging for the amount of packaging on which the logo was placed (and not the amount of packaging collected for recycling) is abuse of a dominant position. The abuse was of double nature: exploitative (by imposing unfair terms and prices) and anti-trust (by preventing DSD contractors from using an alternative system). The behaviour of DSD went beyond the scope of the 'essential function of the trade mark right' (which is indicating to consumers that they can return the packaging within the DSD system). Hence there was no basis for charging fees for collecting packaging in another way.[124]

120 See Ch. Stothers, *CFI upholds 'compulsory licenses' of Green Dot trade mark*, (2007) 2 (10) Journal of Intellectual Property Law & Practice 653; *idem*, *ECJ upholds 'compulsory licenses' of Green Dot trade mark*, (2009) 4 (12) Journal of Intellectual Property Law & Practice 855.

121 ECJ Case C-385/07 P of 16 July 2009; Ch. Stothers, *ECJ upholds 'compulsory licenses' of Green Dot trade mark*, (2009) 4 (12) Journal of Intellectual Property Law & Practice 855.

122 The facts of the case after Ch. Stothers, *CFI upholds 'compulsory licenses' of Green Dot trade mark*, (2007) 2 (10) Journal of Intellectual Property Law & Practice, 2007 653.

123 Cases T-151/01, ECR 2007, II-01607, and T-289/01, ECR 2007, II-01691.

124 The rule "no service, no fee"; cf. M. Gremminger, G. Miersch, *The Court of First Instance confirms Duales System Deutschland's abuse of dominance in the packaging re-*

In the second case the Commission concluded that competitors had not been allowed to offer a service, in particular because they could not use the same containers for the purpose. What was abusive was that householders accepted only one container for a given kind of waste products[125].

In the appeal DSD stated in particular that by imposing the gratuitous compulsory license the Commission violated TRIPS and the principal function of a trade mark – its distinctive function. The first of the objections was set aside by the CFI stating that it did not impose a compulsory license but only determined more restrictive terms for the license granted by DSD[126]. As for the second objection the CFI reasoned that the Green Dot mark does not tell consumers the origin of the goods but in fact only informs that a product bearing the mark can be recycled through the DSD system. As a result the decision of the Commission does not cause any disproportionate impairment of the trade right mark (or at least does not cause an impairment which is not justified by the necessity to prevent abuse of a dominant position)[127]. This position was upheld by the ECJ in its already mentioned decision of 2009. It is emphasized that the relevant state of affairs was absolutely exceptional and, therefore, the decisions cannot be interpreted as an indication that undertakings are compelled by anti-trust agencies to grant third parties the use of their trade marks[128].

The Green Dot mark was also subject of proceedings before national competition authorities. For example, the Bulgarian Commission for Protection of Competition concluded that the licensee abused its dominant position on the Bulgarian territory among other things by refusing to sub-license the right to use the mark to competitors. However, the Supreme Administrative Court handed down this decision by a majority vote on 9 February 2007[129].

(b) There are numerous cases of unwarranted encroachment on the trade mark rights concerning pharmaceuticals re-packaging. Such an encroachment have its legal basis in the provisions of Arts. 28 and 30 TWE (now Arts. 34 and 36 TFEU), although Art. 82 TWE (now Art. 102 TFEU) can also be applied. The fundamental normative difference between these two provisions is that Art. 102 TFEU prohibits abuse of a dominant position while Art. 32 and 36 protect the

cycling system, 2007 (3) Competition Policy Newsletter 47; Ch. Stothers (*supra* note 121), p. 653 f.

125 Ch. Stothers (*supra* note 121), p. 654.

126 Ch. Stothers (*supra* note 120), p. 855 et seqq.

127 Cf. M. Gremminger, G. Miersch (*supra* note 123), p. 48 f.

128 Ch. Stothers (*supra* note 121), p. 654.

129 Cf. D. Fessenko, *The Bulgarian Supreme Administrative Court handed down an NCA decision finding that a holder of the trade mark "Der Grüne Punkt" abused its dominant position on the collective waste management market (Ecopack Bulgaria)*, e-Competitions, May 2007, p. 1.

free movement of goods. They are also targeted differently: Art. 30 covers the competence of Member States introducing IP-protecting regulations while Art. 102 TFEU applies to individual market behaviour of undertakings and their impact on competition[130]. The specific subject-matter is related to the problem of the free movement of goods[131]. However, whether permission to encroach on intellectual property rights is based on Art. 36 or on Art. 102 TFEU, the result is the compulsory encroachment on the exclusivity of the right holder. In each of the two cases the situation will be subject to the examination of its compliance with the quoted TRIPS provisions.

Let us begin by pointing out that when a product bearing a trade mark is introduced into circulation on the territory of the EU, either by the right holder or following his consent, the exhaustion of the rights to the mark arises from the right holder's inability to oppose the circulation of the product within the Community. In the case of the medicinal products the situation is a little more complicated since, due to the notification requirement and the possible differences in the name used, the imported product cannot be frequently introduced into circulation in its original packaging. Re-packaging consists in re-labelling or in substituting the original packaging with a new one (or, to be more precise, in putting the packaging that comes from the manufacturer into a new exterior packaging of the importer called re-boxing) [132].

Re-packaging conflicts with the exclusive right of a brand owner to place a trade mark on a product because the parallel importer usually places his trade mark on the packaged product again[133]. Under Art. 7(2) of Council Directive 89/104/EEC of 21 December 1988, a brand owner is entitled to prohibit the use of his trade mark by third parties on goods sold in the Community '[...] where there exist legitimate reasons [...], especially where the condition of the goods is changed or impaired after they have been put on the market'[134]. Re-packaging may constitute a 'legitimate' reason for a brand owner to oppose further market-

130 Cf. J. Viniol (*supra* notes 8 and 1), p. 87 and *ibidem*, note 23.

131 Cf. J. Viniol (*supra* notes 8 and 1), p. 87.

132 Cf. Re-packaging of medicines in Europe, European Association of Euro-Pharmaceutical Companies, September 2007, available at: http://www.eaepc.org/ admin/files/re-packaging_of_medicines.pdf.

133 Cf. R. Skubisz, *Import równoległy produktów leczniczych w zmienionych opakowaniach a ochrona znaków towarowych (w świetle orzecznictwa Trybunału Sprawiedliwości Wspólnot Europejskich),* 100 ZNUJ 421 (2007).

134 *Re-packaging of pharmaceutical products by parallel importers: ECJ's judgment in Case C-348/04 Boehringer Ingelheim and Others v. Swingward and Others*, Brussels 2007, p. 1 note 3.

ing of re-packaged pharmaceutical products.[135] In particular cases, however, the courts ruled in favour of re-packaging by a third party. Later I will discuss the key decisions relevant to the matter.

In the 1978 *Hoffmann-La Roche & Co. AG v. Centrafarm Vertriebsgesellschaft Pharmazeutischer Erzeugnisse GmbH*[136] case the ECJ indicated the following criteria for authorization of re-packaging, stating that prevention of marketing constitutes a disguised restriction on trade between Member States within the meaning of the second sentence of Art. 36 (now 36 TFEU) of the treaty where:

- it is established that the use of the trade-mark right by the proprietor, having regard to the marketing system which he has adopted, will contribute to the artificial partitioning of the markets between Member States;
- it is shown that re-packaging cannot adversely affect the original condition of the product;
- the proprietor of the mark receives prior notice of the marketing of the re-packaged product; and
- it is stated on the new packaging by whom the product has been re-packaged.[137]

In the 1996 *Bristol-Myers Squibb e.a. v. Paranova*[138] case the ECJ stated that the trademark owner may not 'legitimately oppose' re-packaging of a pharmaceutical product if:

- repacking is necessary to market the product in the country of importation;
- it does not affect the original condition of the product inside the packaging;
- the new packaging clearly states who re-packaged the product and the name of manufacturer;
- the presentation of the re-packaged product is not liable to damage the reputation of the trademark or of its owner; and
- the importer gives notice to the trademark owner before the re-packaged product is put on sale, and, on demand, supplies him with a specimen of the re-packaged product.[139]

135 *Re-packaging of pharmaceutical products by parallel importers: ECJ's judgment in Case C-348/04 Boehringer Ingelheim and Others v. Swingward and Others*, Brussels 2007, p. 1.

136 ECR 1978, 1139.

137 Judgment of the Court of 23 May 1978, Case 102/77, ECR 1978, 01139 – *Hoffman-La Rohe Co. AG v. Centrafarm Vertriebsgesellschaft Pharmaceutischer Erzeugnisse mbH.*

138 Joined cases C-427/93, C-429/93 and C-436/93, ECR 1996, I-3457 – *Bristol-Myers Squibb e.a. v. Paranova.*

139 H. Armengod, L. M. Baudenbacher, *The Re-packaging of Pharmaceutical Products and Parallel Trade in the EU,* RAJ Pharma, December 2009, p. 783.

The ‘necessity’ and ‘notice’ requirements were brought up in a 2002 case.[140] The ECJ concluded that

- pursuant to Art. 7(2) of the Trade Marks Directive, a trade mark owner is entitled to rely on its trade mark rights in order to prevent a parallel importer from re-packaging pharmaceutical products unless the exercise of those rights contributes to artificial partitioning of the market;
- replacement packaging of pharmaceutical products will be "necessary" if, taking into account the circumstances in an importing member state, without such re-packaging, effective access to the market, or a substantial part of the market, in that member state is considered to be hindered due to strong resistance from a significant proportion of consumers to re-labelled pharmaceutical products, and
- in order to be entitled to re-package and market a trade marked pharmaceutical product, a parallel importer must give prior notice to the trade mark owner that it intends to do so.[141]

In a 1997 case[142] the ETS pointed out that using trade marks the right holder may not cause artificial partitioning of the markets between member states which happens especially when the purpose of re-packaging is to fulfil a legal obligation or to attain important objectives which are legitimate under Community law. However, the fact that a proprietor of trade mark rights makes use of those rights to prevent a third party from removing and then re-affixing or replacing labels bearing his trade mark in order to remove those numbers does not contribute to an artificial partitioning of the markets between Member States; It has been shown that

- the re-labelling cannot affect the original condition of the product;
- the presentation of the re-labelled product is not such as to be liable to damage the reputation of the trade mark and its owner; and
- the person who re-labels the products informs the trade mark owner of the re-labelling before the re-labelled products are put on a sale.

Next in a 2007 case (*Boehringer II*) the ECJ, answering the question concerning the interpretation of the BMS conditions, namely the issue of the ‘necessity’ of

140 Judgment of the Court of 23 April 2002, Case C-143/00, ECR 2002, I-3759 – *Boehringer Ingelheim and Others v. Swingward and Others*.

141 N. L. Lehmann, *Clarification needed over grey goods in Europe*, Managing Intellectual Property (IP Focus 2009 Brand Management), May 2009, p. 3.

142 Judgment of the Court of 11 November 1997, Case C-349/95, ECR 1997, I-06227 – *Frits Loendersloot, trading as F. Loendersloot Internationale Expeditie v. George Ballantine & Son Ltd and Others*.

the burden of proof and the consequence of the failure to notify the brand owner about re-packaging[143] concluded that

- re-labelling poses the same risks to the mark owner as re-boxing in the term of potentially undermining the guarantee of origin and thereby confirming that all the five BMS conditions also apply not only to re-boxing but also to re-labelling.
- the condition that the re-packaging of the pharmaceutical product be necessary for its further commercialisation in the importing member state is directed solely at the fact of re-packaging and not at the manner and style of the re-packaging.
- the condition that the presentation of the pharmaceutical product must not be such as to be liable to damage the reputation of the trade mark and of its owner is not restrained to cases where the re-packaging is defective, of poor quality, or untidy.
- it is a question of fact for the national court to decide in the light of the circumstances of each case whether the fact that a parallel importer fails to affix the trade mark to the new exterior carton ("de-branding"), or applies either his own logo or house-style or get-up or a get-up used for a number of different products ("co-branding"), or positions the additional label so as wholly or partially to obscure the owner's trade mark, or fails to state on the additional label that the trade mark in question belongs to the owner, or prints the name of the parallel importer in capital letters, is liable to damage the trade mark's reputation.
- where it is established that the pharmaceutical products have been re-packaged, it is for the parallel importer to prove the existence of the BMS conditions which, if fulfilled, will prevent the trade mark owner from opposing further commercialization of the trade marked pharmaceutical products.
- a parallel importer who fails to give prior notice to the trade mark owner will infringe the rights of those owners by subsequently importing re-packaged products, so long as the owner has not received notice from that parallel importer.[144]

The decision was criticized for not answering the primary question, i.e. what causes damage to the reputation of a trade mark or its owner. It was stated that failure to indicate relevant practical criteria for establishing damage to a mark will give birth to incessant disputes[145].

143 N. L. Lehmann (*supra* note 140), p. 3.
144 *Ibidem.*
145 *Ibidem.*

In a 2008 verdict[146] the ECJ regarded the issue in the following way:

> 1. Art. 7(2) of Council Directive 89/104/EEC of 21 December 1988 to approximate the laws of the Member States relating to trade marks, as amended by the Agreement on the European Economic Area of 2 May 1992, is to be interpreted as meaning that, where it is established that re-packaging of the pharmaceutical product is necessary for further marketing in the Member State of importation, the presentation of the packaging should be assessed only against the condition that it should not be such as to be liable to damage the reputation of the trade mark or that of its proprietor.
>
> 2. The said Art. 7(2) of the Directive is to be interpreted as meaning that it is for the parallel importer to furnish to the proprietor of the trade mark the information which is necessary and sufficient to enable the latter to determine whether the re-packaging of the product under that trade mark is necessary in order to market it in the Member State of importation.

5.3 Conclusions

The community law does not provide for use of rights under registered trade marks for the purpose of abusing the dominant position or preventing a free movement of goods. The *Green Dot* case was special insofar as the mark did in fact serve the function of distinguishing goods of one undertaking from those of another. Indeed, the right holder may not have used the trade mark.[147]

III. General conclusions

A grant of a compulsory license under the anti-trust law may take place only in exceptional circumstances, on case-by-case basis. In my opinion the decisions issued by courts so far do not draw a clear guideline but settle specific cases that are hard to generalize. It is a fact that in the cases discussed the circumstances were exceptional.

Some verdicts on copyright infringement (*Magill, IMS*) may raise principled doubts as to whether exclusive rights were as a matter of fact infringed. But with respect to the *Green Dot* case it is not certain whether the owner of the mark was using it in the meaning of the trade mark law.

If IP laws contain instruments that counteract abuse of those laws then granting compulsory licenses under the anti-trust law is quite restrained and perhaps even unnecessary. This regards patent law (where there are broad-scope provi-

146 Judgment of the Court (2nd Chamber) of 22 December 2008, Case C-276/05, OJ EC C 44 of 21 February 2009, p. 2 – *The Wellcome Foundation Ltd v. Paranova Pharmazeutika Handels GmbH.*

147 Cf. Case C 48/05, *ECR* 2007, I-1017 – *Adam Opel AG v. Autec AG.*

sions for the compulsory encroachment on the exclusivity of the right holder) and the design law (after the introduction the so-called repairs clause).

The compulsory licenses provisions in the IP law contribute to the increase of legal certainty in particular because they are *ex ante* grants, following a certain procedure.

Compulsory Patent Licences under German Law

Horst-Peter Götting

I. *Introduction*

Compulsory patent licences contravene with two corresponding overriding principles: On the one hand the principle that a patent is an exclusive right and on the other hand the principle of freedom of contract.

It lies in the very nature of a patent as a property right that it allows the patentee to exclude others for making use of the protected invention. And it is the backbone of civil law that reflects the model of a free market oriented society that the right holder enjoys the freedom to decide if or on which conditions he is prepared to conclude a contract with another party allowing her to benefit from the invention.

Basically, a patent gives a patentee the power to act as a monopolist if the market allows it and enables him to hold production of his invention down to the level of maximum profit.[1] But German law along with the law of other countries and in line with the international legal framework and the development of European case law has established a regime of compulsory licences which under certain circumstances prevents the patentee from acting as a sole producer.[2] Instead he will be confronted with direct competition subject only to a royalty or other fee on the licensee's sales.[3]

In other words: The compulsory licence is designed to limit the exclusive rights of the patentee in order to promote competition. But against the background of the principles described above, i.e. the exclusivity resulting from a patent and the freedom of contract, it is necessary that very strong policy reasons can be put forward to interfere with the rights of the patentee.

In general, compulsory contracts are taken into consideration in cases of monopolies in various areas. In Germany the obligation to conclude a contract is imposed upon public institutions or private undertakings on the basis of specific legislation or the general clauses of civil or antitrust law if there is a dependence on goods or services referring to basic needs, for instance food, healthcare, public transportation, supply with energy, etc.

1 Cornish, Llewelyn and Aplin, *Intellectual Property*, 7th ed. (2010), 7-40.
2 *Ibidem*.
3 *Ibidem*.

With regard to patents it has to be taken into account that they usually establish a monopoly only in a legal but not in an economic sense. Patents grant an exclusive right in so far as they allow the patentee to exclude others from the exploitation of the protected invention. But in general they do not bring about an absolute dependence because alternative solutions are available lying outside of the scope of the patent protection and can be used as substitutes. Monopoly in an economic sense resulting from a patent is a rare exception. It may arise if at the time being the invention is unique, is a "pioneer" invention of such a considerable economic importance and value that deviating technological solutions are not in sight.

But even such an exceptional situation does not automatically justify a right to claim a compulsory licence. It is in the very nature of patents that they restrict competition and may even entail an economic monopoly. The exclusivity resulting from a patent is not the exception of competition but its instrument. It applies the paradox: "Promotion of competition through the restriction of competition".[4] The function of patents to serve as a reward and as an incentive for the inventor that may restrict competition during the term of patent protection is expected to stimulate and foster competition in the long run.

To put it quite simple: Without the monopoly granted by patent protection the motivation to invest in technological innovation would be diminished. This philosophy of patent law is marked by economic considerations that stand in close context to the antitrust law. It is a permanent task for the legislator and the courts to strike a balance between the freedom of competition and the exclusive right of the patentee.

A retrospective look at the historical development shows that patent law and antitrust law are intertwined.

II. Historical background

The *Statute of Monopolies* which is deemed to be the first patent legislation in a modern sense and the "Magna Carta" of the patent system was not a monopoly but an "anti-monopoly" regulation.[5] It was directed against the arbitrary practice of King James I. rewarding his political creditors with trading monopolies granted by letters patent. The statute generally prohibited monopolies and only exceptionally allowed patent monopolies for 14 years upon "any manner of new manufacture" within the realm to the "true and first inventor". It contained also a

4 Götting, *Gewerblicher Rechtsschutz*, 9th ed. (2010), § 6 marginal note 27.

5 Götting (*supra* note 4), § 2 marginal notes 18 et seq.; Cornish, Llewelyn and Aplin (*supra* note 1), 3-04 et seq.

provision against misuses by stating that the protected manufactures were not to be "contrary to the law nor mischievous to the State, by raising prices of commodities at home, or hurt of trade, or generally inconvenient".[6]

In Germany in the course of the vivid debate preceding the enactment of the First Federal Patent Law in 1877 there was an anti-patent movement.[7] The opponents of the establishment of a patent system argued that the monopoly conferred on the patentee would have detrimental effects on the freedom of competition. The line of compromise intending to reconcile the antagonistic positions was reached by the acknowledgment of a compulsory licence that can be requested if the requirement of a sufficient public interest is fulfilled.

Before focusing on the latest developments in Germany it appears to be appropriate to sketch quite briefly the legal framework on the International and European level in which German law is more or less embedded.

III. International law

1. Paris Convention[8]

Art. 5 A (2) state the principle that every member state is free to take legal measures providing a grant of compulsory licences in order to prevent abuses which may result from the exercise of the rights conferred by the patent.

2. TRIPS[9]

Art. 31 TRIPS allows the grant of a compulsory licence (or any other use without the patentees authorisation) on various grounds that have to be assessed in light of the specific circumstances of every individual case.

6 Cornish, Llewelyn and Aplin (*supra* note 1), 3-05.

7 Götting (*supra* note 4), § 2 marginal notes 40 et seq.

8 Paris Convention for the Protection of Industrial Property.

9 Agreement on Trade Related Aspects of Intellectual Property Rights.

1. The case law of the European Court of Justice

Leaving aside the special regulation on compulsory licences for pharmaceutical products, there are no explicit provisions in community law addressing the issue of compulsory licences in general. The legal basis for answering the question whether a compulsory licence for an intellectual property right has to be granted is the general clause of European competition law in Art. 102 TFEU[10] (ex-Art. 82 EC), prohibiting an abuse of a dominant position by an undertaking.

In its case law the European Court of Justice has developed the relevant criteria to determine whether the refusal to licence constitutes an abuse of a dominant position triggering an obligation to licence. Although the decisions of the court concern design or copyright law the reasoning on which they are based give also an orientation for the assessment of compulsory licensing in patent law.

The leading case is still the famous *Magill* decision of 1995 that has outlined the essential criteria to which also later decisions recur.[11] The starting point of the grounds of the Magill judgment is the following statement: "The refusal to grant a licence, even if it is the act of an undertaking holding a dominant position, cannot in itself constitute abuse of a dominant position". But the court continues: "However, the exercise of an exclusive right by a proprietor may, in exceptional circumstances involve abusive conduct".

The requirement of "exceptional circumstances" is met if the refusal to grant the licence (1) prevents the appearance of a new product for which there is potential consumer demand; (2) the refusal is not justified and (3) the dominant undertaking reserves for itself the secondary market by excluding all competition on that market since it denies access to basic information which is indispensible for the appearance of the new product in question.

It is generally assumed that the requirement of a "new product" plays the decisive role as it is a key factor of the assessment whether the condition of "exceptional circumstances is fulfilled". This standpoint has been confirmed also in the *IMS* judgment of 2004.[12]

10 Treaty on the Functioning of the European Union.

11 Joined Cases C-241 and 241/91 P, ECR 1995, I-743 = 27 IIC 78 (1996) - *Radio Telefis Eireann v. Commission (Magill)*.

12 ECJ of 29 April 2004, Case C-418/01, 35 IIC 564 (2004) - *IMS Health*.

2. European Commission

The "DG Competition Discussion Paper on the Application of Art. 82 of the Treaty to Exclusionary Abuses" submitted by the European Commission in 2005 follows the principles laid down by the European Court of Justice on the one hand.[13] But on the other hand it goes even beyond the ruling of the court as it extends the abuse of a dominant position of an undertaking by a refusal to licence an intellectual property right also to the primary market.

The relevant parts of the discussion paper read as follows:

"The refusal to licence an intellectual property therefore does not in itself constitute an abuse. Only under exceptional circumstances can the refusal to licence an IPR be considered an abuse"[14] ... "This may only be the case if the undertaking which requests the licence does not intend to limit itself essentially to duplicating the goods or services already offered on this market by the owner of the IPR, but intends to produce new goods or services not offered by the owner of the right and for which there is a potential consumer demand." ... "A refusal to licence an IPR protected technology which is indispensable as a basis for follow-on innovation by competitors may be abusive even if the licence is not sought to directly incorporate the technology in clearly identifiable new goods and services. The refusal of licensing an IPR protected technology should not impair consumers' ability to benefit from innovation brought about by the dominant undertaking's competitors."[15]

As a consequence according to the opinion of the commission, expressed in the discussion paper, the refusal to licence an IPR can be considered an abuse even if the technology for which the licence is sought will not bring about new products or services. In so far the commission deviates from the "new product" requirement of the court.

13 *"Discussion Paper on the Application of Art. 82 of the Treaty to Exclusionary Abuses"*, December 2005, available at: http://ec.europa.eu/comm/competition/antitrust/others/discpaper2005.pdf.

14 *L.c.* at p. 67.

15 *L.c.* at p. 68.

1. Compulsory licensing according to Sec. 24 Patent Act

In German law Sec. 24 Patent Act provides for the grant of a compulsory licence. As already pointed out in the historical retrospective the introduction of a regulation of compulsory licensing was the result of a compromise between the advocates and the opponents of the establishment of a patent system in Germany. It was designed to function as a corrective, as a countervailing factor and should compensate or at least mitigate the potential anticompetitive effects caused by a patent for a key technology.

However, in practice the indispensible condition of a "public interest" turned out to be an insurmountable obstacle. In the past five decades, some 40 requests for compulsory licences were filed with the Federal Patent Court and in only one case in 1991 did the Federal Patent Court grant a compulsory licence.[16] But this decision was quashed by the Federal Court of Justice.[17]

Thus, it can be said, that compulsory licensing on the basis of Sec. 24 Patent Act has no practical significance.[18] Against this background the focus shifted from patent law to antitrust law.

2. Compulsory licences on the basis of antitrust law

For a long time an interface between patent law and antitrust law has been principally denied in Germany. It prevailed the "inherency doctrine", according to which intellectual property law defines the scope of protection and competition and antitrust law must not interfere. As a consequence of the view that patents are immune from competition law intervention the provision on compulsory licensing in Sec. 24 of the Patent Act was considered to be a conclusive lex specialis excluding the application of antitrust law.[19]

16 BPatG of 7 June 1991, Case 4 Li 1/90 (EU), BPatGE 32, 184.

17 BGH of 5 December 1995, Case X ZR 26/92, BGHZ 131, 247 = 28 IIC 242 (1997) - *Polyferon (Compulsory License)*.

18 See Kraßer, *Patentrecht*, p. 834 (6th ed. 2009).

19 In particular the so called Doctrine of Essential facilities did not found acceptance. According to Sec. 19 (4) No. 4 Law Against Restraints of Competition, it is an abuse of dominance when the dominant undertaking for goods or services refuses another undertaking access to its own network or infrastructure facilities at reasonable prices, without the shared use of which it is de facto or de jure impossible for the latter to compete against the dominant undertaking in the upstream or downstream market. The legislator made clear, that it is not the purpose of this provision to establish a right to use others in-

In a groundbreaking decision issued in 2004, called "Standard Tight-Head Drum" the Federal Court of Justice clearly rejected this interpretation and signalled a reversal of direction.[20] The case concerned the question whether a different treatment that lies in the grant of some paid licences and some free licences for a patent is an unlawful abuse of a dominant position or a discrimination in the sense of Secs. 19, 20 (1) Act Against Restraints of Competition.

With regard to the applicability of antitrust provisions the court made quite clear that "a competition law claim to the grant of a patent licence that has come about as a result of abuse of a market-dominating position, and unfair restraint or discrimination is not ruled out by the fact that the patent court has the authority to allocate a compulsory licence under Sec. 24 of the Patent Act."

The court argues that the provision on compulsory licences in Sec. 24 Patent Act and the competition law provisions of an abuse of dominant positions in Secs. 19 and 20 Act Against Restraints of Competition follow different objectives and operate in different circumstances. Whereas patent law requires the public interest, the claim in competition law, by contrast, serves to enforce the prohibition on abuse of a market-dominating position that applies to every market participant.[21]

With respect to the circumstances under which compulsory licence can successfully be claimed the Federal Court of Justice has laid down the following principle:

"Given an industry standard or standard-like general conditions that force would-be entrants to a downstream market to adhere to the technical specifications of a patent, a market-dominating patent proprietor is in breach of the anti-discrimination provision when he exploits this situation to restrict access to that market by applying criteria for granting licences that contradict the purpose of the Act Against Restraints of Competition to guarantee freedom of competition."[22]

It is surprising that the Federal Court of Justice did not deal with Art. 82 EC-Treaty and the "new product" requirement that has been developed by the European Court of Justice. It seems that the decision deviated from this conception and follows a broader economic approach focusing on genuine indispensability for competition by substitution in a downstream market and non-justifiability of the refusal to licence by objective economic reasons. This seems to be in line

tellectual property rights, see response of German Federal Government in BT-Drucks. 13/9720.

20 BGH of 13 July 2004, Case KZR 40/02, 36 IIC 741 (2005) - *Standard Tight-Head Drum (Standardspundfass)*.

21 *L.c.* at p. 744.

22 *L.c.* at p. 746.

with the stance taken by the commission in the discussion paper, mentioned above.

Such a method of an all embracing analysis scrutinizing the pro and anti competitive factors involved may well lead to convincing results. But it cannot be overlooked that it causes considerable legal uncertainty because it is difficult for the parties to anticipate the outcome.

In a recent judgment, delivered in June 2009, the Federal Court of Justice ruled that the obligation to grant a compulsory licence can be raised as a defence and counterclaim against a prohibitory injunction based on an action for patent infringement.[23] However, it is a necessary prerequisite that the defendant has submitted to the plaintiff an unconditional offer to conclude a licence contract and to pay an appropriate licence fee.

VI. Conclusion

In summing up it can be stated that there is a complex interface and interplay between patent law and antitrust law. The "inherency doctrine" prevailing for a long time in Germany according to which the scope of protection resulting from a patent is immune from any intervention of competition law cannot be maintained any longer, but has become obsolete.

Instead antitrust law functions as an ultimate tool, a last resort to curb in exceptional cases where patents entail an economic monopoly with counterproductive excesses of the immanent anti-competitive effects of the patent system. If a patent does not promote but prevent promotion of technological innovation it fails to attain its objective. The corrective role that competition law plays in order to achieve this objective may lead to the establishment of an Intellectual Property Antitrust Law.

23 BGH of 6 May 2009, Case KZR 39/06, 41 IIC 369 (2010) - *Orange Book Standard.*

The Defences of Non-Use and Genericness in Trade Mark Litigation

Philipp Hanske

A. Introduction

Trade mark litigation can be a venturesome undertaking for trade mark proprietors, since the alleged infringer of a registered trade mark has a number of defences at hand which may result in a deletion of the mark. Two of them will be discussed in this paper: the defences of non-use and genericness, both enshrined in Art. 51 of the Community Trade Mark Regulation 2009[1] (CTMR). Both defences deal with situations in which the trade mark proprietor has in one way or another neglected his obligations, either because he has not used it adequately or because he has not defended it adequately. After giving a short overview on how these defences can be introduced into a trade mark dispute, this paper will turn to the question, which extent and type of use is necessary to avoid revocation of a trade mark based on non-use. Thereafter the paper will enquire in which case genericness can be established, and which actions a trade mark owner has to take in order to avoid his trade mark from becoming a generic term.

B. Introducing the Defences of Non-Use and Genericness into Trade Mark Litigation

An alleged infringer of a trade mark that is liable to be revoked because of non-use or genericness is not required to wait until the case is taken to court by the trade mark owner. In the Community trade mark system the rights in a trade mark can be declared to be revoked because of non-use or genericness upon application to the Trade Marks and Designs Registration Office of the EU (OHIM).[2] The same applies to trade marks registered under the German Trade Marks Act (MarkenG).[3] In this case the application has to be filed with the Ger-

1 Council Regulation (EC) No. 207/2009 of 26 February 2009 on the Community Trade Mark, OJ EU L 78 of 24 March 2009, p. 1.
2 Art. 51 (1) (a) and (b) CTMR.
3 Sec. 49 (1) and (2) MarkenG.

man Patent and Trade Mark Office (DPMA).[4] In addition a German trade mark can be challenged in a separate lawsuit.[5] Every natural person or legal entity is entitled to initiate the three aforementioned proceedings.[6]

Once faced with court actions for trade mark infringement the defendant can introduce the defences of non-use and genericness into those proceedings. If the claimant is relying on a Community trade mark, the defendant can base a counterclaim on non-use and genericness.[7] In this case the domestic Community trade mark court has the jurisdiction to decide on the revocation of a Community trade mark with effect for the whole Community.[8] If the claimant is relying on a German trade mark a distinction has to be drawn between non-use and genericness. Sec. 25 (1) MarkenG provides that in a case of non-use the owner of a trade mark has no cause of action against a third party. Thus non-use is a defence (an *Einrede* in German legal terminology) and as such within the domain of substantive law. A counterclaim is not required. The MarkenG remains quiet, though, whether a trade mark that has become a generic term can be challenged within infringement proceedings. It is however well recognized that a defendant can base a defence on genericness or choose to introduce the revocation lawsuit of Sec. 55 MarkenG by way of a counterclaim.[9] This understanding is based on the notion that no-one should be able to take legal action relying on a trade mark that is subject to revocation. This notion is rooted back to the overarching principle of equity and good faith enshrined in Secs. 242 and 138 of the German Civil Code.[10] Since the civil courts do have the authority to decide on the revocation based on genericness in the separate proceedings of Sec. 55 MarkenG anyway, no illegitimate shift of authority from the DPMA to the courts takes place.[11] Further there is no reason why the defence of genericness should be treated in a different way than the defence of non-use, since both defences lead to the revocation of a trade mark.

4 Sec. 53 (1) MarkenG.

5 Sec. 55 MarkenG. Such an action is not available for Community trade marks, see R. Ingerl and C. Rohnke, *Markengesetz*, 2nd ed. (2003), at § 55 marginal note 3.

6 Art. 56 (1) (a) CTMR, Secs. 53 (1) and 55 (2) MarkenG; Ingerl and Rohnke (*supra* note 5), at § 49 marginal note 11; F. Hacker in Ströbele/Hacker, *Markengesetz*, 9th ed. (2009), at § 49 marginal note 3.

7 Art. 51 (1) CTMR.

8 Arts. 1 (2), 96 (d), 100 CTMR.

9 BGH 1990 GRUR 37, 38 - *Quelle*; Ingerl and Rohnke (*supra* note 5), at § 49 marginal note 37; F. Hacker (*supra* note 6), at § 14 marginal note 27.

10 Ingerl and Rohnke (*supra* note 5), at § 49 marginal note 37.

11 *Ibidem.*

C. *The Non-Use Defence*

The tenth recital of the CTMR states that "*[t]here is no justification for protecting Community trade marks [...] except where the trade marks are actually used*". This is convincing. Only trade marks that are used are able to communicate information to the consumer and thereby function as indicators of origin.[12] The five year period in which a trade mark has to be used, found in Arts. 15, 42 (2) and 51 (1) (a) CTMR, posses few legal problems, too.[13] A more difficult question to answer is: What is 'use of the mark' within the meaning of these provisions?

I. The Extent of Use

'Use' within the meaning of Art. 51 (1) (a) CTMR should not be confused with 'use' within the meaning of Art. 9 (1) CTMR. Not every act, which qualifies for infringing use would also qualify for use that is sufficient to preserve the trade mark.[14] In the leading decision on the matter, *Ansul v. Ajax Brandbeveiliging*, the European Court of Justice (ECJ) gave the following definition:

> "[...] use of the mark on the market for the goods or services protected by that mark and not just internal use by the undertaking concerned. [...] Use of the mark must therefore relate to goods or services already marketed or about to be marketed and for which preparations by the undertaking to secure customers are under way, particularly in the form of advertising campaigns. Such use may be either by the trade mark proprietor or, as envisaged in Art. 10 (3) of the Directive, by a third party with authority to use the mark."[15]

It can be concluded from these findings that the trade mark owner will be on the save side if he can demonstrate significant sales of goods marked with the sign to the end-user. Pre-release activities, such as advertising campaigns, will only be sufficient if they take place outside the undertaking and directly serve to secure customers. Further it is not required to show actual profit-making with the goods

12 L. Bently and B. Sherman, *Intellectual Property Law*, 3rd ed. (2009), at p. 894.

13 For an overview see: Ingerl and Rohnke (*supra* note 5), at § 49 marginal notes 7-9; Bently and Sherman (*supra* note 12), at p. 895. An interesting question that was raised was whether the five year period could be circumvented by registering the same trade mark twice. In *Origins Natural Resources v. Origin Clothing* the High Court of Justice of England & Wales answered that question in the affirmative. See 1995 FSR 280, *per* Jacob J at 284.

14 Bently and Sherman (*supra* note 12), at p. 896; P. Ströbele in Ströbele/Hacker, *Markengesetz*, at § 26 marginal note 13.

15 ECJ, Case C-40/01, 2003 ECR I-2439 = 2003 GRUR 425, at para 37 - *Ansul v. Ajax Brandbeveiliging*.

or services protected; especially if the owner is a charitable organisation.[16] If, however, the mark is affixed to items, which are given free of charge as a reward for the purchase of other goods, use will not be established with regards to those free items, since their distribution does not serve to secure a share in the market for goods in the same class as those free items.[17]

1. The Objective and Subjective Approach in Assessing Use

In many cases, however, the trade mark owner has used the trade mark only to a limited extent. Either he has not generated large sales of his products marked with the sign, or he has stopped producing these products, but continued to provide customer support, and offer accessories or spare parts for them. In these cases it is questionable whether the mentioned activities amount to use within the meaning of Art. 51 (1) (a) CTMR.

In the English version of the CTMR the trade mark owner is required to show 'genuine use'. Other language versions use slightly different terms, such as 'ernsthaft' (German) or 'serieux' (French), which could both be translated into 'serious', and 'rzeczywiście' (Polish), 'normaal' (Dutch) and 'verkligt' (Swedish), which are again less subjective terms than those in the German or French version. Maybe because of these differences it was debated whether an objective or subjective approach should be applied. Objective genuineness would have required the trade mark owner to show a substantial use of his trade mark.[18] In contrast, subjective genuineness would have required the trade mark owner to show honest use, which may be *de minimis*, but may also not be accomplished if there is large-scale use solely as part of a trade mark protection programme.[19] In *Ansul v. Ajax Brandbeveiliging*[20] and *La Mer v. Goëmar*[21] the ECJ held in favour of a subjective approach. This means that 'token' use, which is use that is only made in order to uphold the registration does not qualify.[22]

According to the ECJ

16 ECJ, Case C-442/07, 2009 GRUR Int. 324, at para. 16 - *Radetzky-Orden v. BKFR*; BGH 2006 WRP 102, 104 - *Gallup*.

17 ECJ, Case C-495/07, 2009 GRUR 410, at para. 21 - *Silberquelle v. Maselli*.

18 Bently and Sherman, (*supra* note 12), at p. 899.

19 *Ibidem*.

20 ECJ, Case C-40/01, 2003 ECR I-2439 = 2003 GRUR 425 - *Ansul v. Ajax Brandbeveiliging*.

21 ECJ, Case C-259/02, 2004 ECR I-1159 - *La Mer v. Goëmar*.

22 *Ansul v. Ajax Brandbeveiliging* (*supra* note 20), at para. 36; P. Ströbele (*supra* note 14), at § 26 marginal note 6.

> "[…] regard must be had to all the facts and circumstances relevant to establishing whether the commercial exploitation of the mark is real, in particular whether such use is viewed as warranted in the economic sector concerned to maintain or create a share in the market for the goods or services protected by the mark."[23]

Since it depends on the individual circumstances of the products or services and their market, the ECJ finds that use does not always need to be quantitatively significant in order to be genuine.[24] If, for example, the product to which the mark is attached is only directed towards a very small market, insignificant sales to a limited group of customers may still be 'genuine use' of that mark. In the case of *La Mer v. Goëmar* sales in a single member state, to a single agent in the range of 800 GBP were considered 'genuine use' by the domestic court, after having taken the ECJ's decision into account.[25] Though the subjective approach might result in such borderline cases once in a while, the objective approach would not have been able to exclude use which is merely made to uphold the registration. Such use is not able to serve the essential function of a trade mark, which is to enable the consumer to distinguish the goods of one undertaking from those of another. The ECJ was therefore right to dismiss the objective approach.

2. The Relevance of After-Sales Activities

Ansul v. Ajax Brandbeveiliging is a very helpful decision for it also provides guidance concerning the evaluation of after-sales activities, such as customer support and the sale of accessories and spare parts. Very often, as can be seen in the cars or electronics industries, these activities continue for years after the production of the original product has been ceased. The ECJ holds that under certain circumstances 'genuine use' of a mark may still be established even though the goods for which it is registered are not available anymore.[26] This will be the case when the trade mark owner continues to sell parts of the product which are "*integral to the make-up or structure of the goods previously sold*" and which bear the mark in question.[27] Further genuine use can also take the form of using the trade mark for goods and services which are "*directly related to those goods and intended to meet the needs of customers of those goods*".[28] According to the ECJ

23 *Ansul v. Ajax Brandbeveiliging* (*supra* note 20), at para. 38.
24 *La Mer v. Goëmar* (*supra* note 21), at paras. 21-22.
25 *La Mer v. Goëmar* 2005 EWCA Civ 978 (Court of Appeal England & Wales).
26 *Ansul v. Ajax Brandbeveiliging* (*supra* note 20), at para. 40.
27 *Ansul v. Ajax Brandbeveiliging* (*supra* note 20), at para. 41.
28 *Ansul v. Ajax Brandbeveiliging* (*supra* note 20), at para. 42.

this will apply to after-sales services, like repair services and the sale of accessories and related parts.[29]

This generous definition of 'genuine use' seems problematic. More often than not, the consumer will buy the aforementioned products or demand the aforementioned services not because he wants to, but because he has to. If he needs a spare part for his broken product he has usually no choice but to go with the product of the original manufacturer. In this case the trade mark does not always need to fulfil its function as a badge of origin. In addition, if the trade mark owner wants to uphold his trade mark for those types of goods and services he is free to file a trade mark application that explicitly covers them.

II. Use of an Altered Mark

An additional problem arises when trade mark owners alter the signs they use for their goods or services, *e.g.* in order to keep up with marketing fashion changes. Art. 15 (1) (a) CTMR states that "*use of the Community trade mark in a form differing in elements which do not alter the distinctive character of the mark*" still constitutes use. According to the ECJ use in a "*slightly different form from that in which it was registered*" may not alter the distinctive character of the mark.[30] Additional guidance can be found in the Court of First Instance's (CFI) decision *Laboratorios v. OHIM.*[31] Here the CFI finds that where a sign has very little distinctive character even slight modifications can suffice to establish non-use of the original trade mark.[32] In this case the trade mark owner registered the mark "J. Giorgio" but used the signs "Giorgio", "Miss Giorgio" and "Giorgio Line". Since the CFI considered the used element "Giorgio" to be a common name, which has low distinctiveness, use was not established.[33]

More detailed case law can be derived from decisions of the domestic courts. The approach of the German Federal Court of Justice (BGH) is to ask, whether the average consumer would consider the used sign to be the same as the registered sign.[34] In answering this question the BGH takes into account the distinctiveness of both the altered and the unaltered part of the trade mark. If the altered or omitted part is of low distinctiveness, *e.g.* because it is a geographical designation, use may still be established.[35] If, on the other hand, the unaltered part is

29 *Ansul v. Ajax Brandbeveiliging* (*supra* note 20), at para. 42.
30 ECJ, Case C-234/06 P, 2008 ETMR 242, at para. 86 - *Il Ponte Finanziaria SpA v. OHIM.*
31 CFI, Case T-156/01, 2003 ECR II-2789 - *Laboratorios RTB v. OHIM.*
32 *Laboratorios RTB v. OHIM* (*supra* note 31), at para. 44.
33 *Ibidem.*
34 BGH 2002 GRUR 167, 168 - *Bit/Bud*; 2003 GRUR 1047, 1048 - *Kellogg's/Kelly's.*
35 BGH 1997 GRUR 744, 746 - *Ecco I.*

of low distinctiveness, use will usually not be established.[36] The Court of Appeal of England and Wales had the opportunity in *Anheuser-Bush v. Budejovicky Budvar*[37] to provide some guidance on the matter. It asked whether the differences between the used and the registered mark alter the distinctive character of the mark as registered. The court further added that the distinctive character is what makes the mark "*in some degree striking and memorable*".[38] The difference between these three approaches can be considered exiguous as they will almost certainly always arrive at the same solution. From a practical point of view, the Court of Appeal's test seems to be the easiest one to apply, as it asks whether those parts of the trade mark have been changed, which make the mark to some degree striking and memorable.

D. The Genericness Defence

The defence of genericness is another way of how the infringer of a registered trade mark can escape liability because of neglecting behaviour on part of the trade mark proprietor. In this case it is not the failure to use the mark but the failure to defend the mark appropriately, that might bring his litigation to no avail. According to Art. 51 (1) (b) CTMR two requirements need to be fulfilled for a defence based on genericness to be successful. First, the trade mark must have become a 'common name in the trade' for the products or services for which it is registered. Second, this development must be a consequence of acts or the inactivity of the trade mark owner. Each of these two elements will be dealt with in turn.

I. The Generic Term Requirement

Three examples may illustrate that trade marks can indeed turn into generic terms. The former trade mark "Linoleum" was held to be a generic term in an English court decision in as early as 1878.[39] "Walkman" was held to be a generic term by the Austrian Supreme Court in 2002.[40] The most recent example is the dispute between Psion plc as the trade mark owner, and Intel, Inc. and Dell, Inc.

36 BGH 1999 GRUR 498, 499 - *Achterdiek.*

37 Court of Appeal England & Wales 2003 RPC (25) 477 - *Anheuser-Bush v. Budejovicky Budvar.*

38 *Anheuser-Bush v. Budejovicky Budvar* (*supra* note 37), *per* Lord Walker at paras. 43-44.

39 Chancery Division England & Wales (1878) 7 Ch D 834 - *Linoleum Manufacturing v. Nairn.*

40 Austrian Supreme Court 34 IIC 966 (2003) - *Walkman.*

as the alleged infringer who sought revocation of Psion's Community and United States trade marks in the term "Netbook" for laptop computers.[41]

In the old Linoleum case the judge asked a simple question in order to determine genericness: *"I want to know what they are to call it. [...] but I have received no answer;[...] except that they must invent a new name."*[42] Probably this simple test would still be able to solve the vast majority of today's cases.[43] From today's perspective Art. 51 (1) (b) CTMR can be viewed as a counterpart to Art. 7 (1) (a) CTMR. The later Article deals with the absence of distinctive character before and the former Article after the registration of the mark.[44] This means that a trade mark becomes a common name when it has lost its distinctive character.[45]

In *Björnekulla v. Procordia*[46] the ECJ answered the adjuvant question from whose point of view genericness is to be judged. This is an important aspect as in many cases consumers might be more liable then traders to use a trade mark as a descriptive term. Since Art. 51 (1) (b) CTMR speaks of the trade mark having become 'a common name in the trade' it was argued that it should be the perspective of the trader that provides the benchmark for genericness.[47] A similar point of view can be derived from a 1964 decision of the BGH, which holds that a mark is not a generic term as long as a significant part of the public, which can exclusively consist of those who are concerned with the production or distribution of the products, considers it to be an indicator of origin.[48] The ECJ however held that under normal circumstances the assessment should be made from the perspective of the consumer or end-user.[49] According to the ECJ the main function of a trade mark is to guarantee the consumer or end-user the origin of the product or service. It is therefore the consumer whose point of view is relevant.[50] The ECJ is however prepared to allow exceptions where "*features of the product market*" require the perception of the trade to be taken into account as well.[51] It

41 See OHIM Reg. No. 000428250; US Patent and Trademark Office Reg. No. 2404976.

42 *Linoleum Manufacturing v. Nairn* (*supra* note 39), per Fry J. at 836.

43 The *Walkman* case is a good example for this assertion, as the court finds that *"no approximately equivalent alternative concept is available to the said market participants to designate products that compete with the plaintiff's trademark goods; thus the plaintiff's trademark is the only common designation for such goods"*. Austrian Supreme Court 34 IIC 966, 968 (2003).

44 Ingerl and Rohnke (*supra* note 5), at § 49 marginal note 34.

45 ECJ, Case C-145/05, 2006 ECR I-3703 = 2006 GRUR 495, at para. 33 - *Levi Strauss v. Casucci.*

46 ECJ, Case C-371/02, 2004 ECR I-5791 = 2004 GRUR Int. 629 - *Björnekullar Fruktindustrier v. Procordia.*

47 Bently and Sherman (*supra* note 12), at p. 908.

48 BGH 1964 GRUR 458, 460 - *Düssel.*

49 *Björnekullar Fruktindustrier v. Procordia* (*supra* note 46), at para. 25.

50 *Björnekullar Fruktindustrier v. Procordia* (*supra* note 46), at paras. 20-23.

51 *Björnekullar Fruktindustrier v. Procordia* (*supra* note 46), at para. 26.

did not provide any example for such an exceptional product market. Bently and Sherman propose that the market for prescription pharmaceuticals might be such a market, where the perception of the medical profession will be relevant, too.[52] Following the ECJ's decision a rebuttal of the genericness defence cannot solely rely on the fact that the trade considers the mark to be an indicator of origin. Additional evidence will have to be provided in order to show that the point of view of the trade has to be taken into account alongside that of the consumer or end-user.

II. The Fault Requirement

Even if a trade mark has turned into a generic term it will only be subject to revocation if this development is the result of the activities or, probably more important, the inactivity of its owner. The fault requirement is therefore not to be understood as a subjective state of mind, such as intent or negligence,[53] but as objectively measurable failures. From a theoretical point of view it is therefore possible for a trade mark which has become a generic term to stay on the register, as long as its owner is taking all the necessary, though unsuccessful, actions to prevent his mark from losing its distinctive character. The question is how those necessary actions have to look like.

In *Levi Strauss v. Casucci* the ECJ called them the *"requirement of vigilant conduct"*.[54] 'Vigilant conduct' obliges the trade mark owner to not take actions which may cause the trade mark to loose its distinctive character. In addition he is required to take actions against others who are using his trade mark in a way that may lead to a loss of distinctiveness.[55] Art. 10 CTMR, which deals with the reproduction of a Community trade mark in a dictionary, provides one possible way of how a trade mark owner can take action in order to protect his mark from becoming a generic term. It was reported that Google, Inc. has demanded the revision of the verb *"(to) google"* (English) or *"googeln"* (German) with the definition *"to search through the internet"* on a number of standard dictionaries, such as *The Oxford English Dictionary* and *Der Duden*, relying on this Article.[56]

52 Bently and Sherman (*supra* note 12), at p. 909.

53 F. Hacker (*supra* note 6), at § 49 marginal note 31; H.-P. Götting, *Gewerblicher Rechtsschutz*, 9th ed. (2010), at § 57 marginal note 6.

54 ECJ, Case C-145/05, 2006 ECR I-3703 = 2006 GRUR 495, at para. 31 - *Levi Strauss v. Casucci*.

55 *Levi Strauss v. Casucci* (*supra* note 54), at para. 30.

56 Heise Online „Google will richtig „googeln" lassen." http://www.heise.de/newsticker/Google-will-richtig-googeln-lassen--/meldung/76830, accessed 2 September 2009; Stephen Foley "To google or not to google? It's a legal question" The Independent 13

Apart from those special cases 'vigilant conduct' means that a trade mark proprietor has to make use of his exclusive right conferred to him by Art. 9 CTMR and take action 'in due time' in order to prevent third parties from using his trade mark in a way that creates a likelihood of confusion.[57] Such actions have the purpose to preserve the distinctive character of the trade mark.

Trade mark protection campaigns are however not confined to court actions. Especially those trade mark owners, who have created a market leadership, are in danger of having their trade mark turned into a generic term. This is because the consumer will often use such trade marks as a synonym for the whole trade.[58] In order to avoid this from happening, trade mark owners carry out trade mark protection campaigns with their business partners. Typically those campaigns are part of a licence agreement and provide the other party with exact directions on how to use the trade mark.[59] Those directions usually require the other party to use the trade mark as an adjective and not as a verb or a noun. Further they are asked to use the mark always in conjunction with a descriptive noun, *e.g.* Google™ search or Lycra® fibre.[60] The effectiveness of those campaigns is questionable as they only reach out to other businesses and not the consumer or end-user. If a company is trying to reach consumers with such information campaigns it might even be interpreted as if the company itself considers its trade mark to be on the brink of genericness.[61] In such a case those policing activities may also be construed to the disadvantage of the trade mark owner.[62] One solution would be to simply abolish the requirement of fault. In this case every "generisised" trade mark would have to be revoked notwithstanding the activities or inactivity of its owner. The problem, however, is that in many cases a trade mark has lost its distinctiveness because of infringing actions of third parties. In these cases it seems difficult to justify the annulment of a property right only due to infringing activities of competitors.

August 2006 http://www.independent.co.uk/news/business/news/to-google-or-not-to-google-its-a-legal-question-411600.html, accessed 2 September 2009.

57 *Levi Strauss v. Casucci* (*supra* note 54), at para. 34.

58 Ingerl and Rohnke (*supra* note 5), at § 49 marginal note 34.

59 A fine example can be found in Google Inc.'s "Guidelines for Third Party Use of Google Brand Features" http://www.google.com/permissions/guidelines.html, accessed 2 September 2009.

60 Google Inc. "Guidelines for Third Party Use of Google Brand Features" http://www.google.com/permissions/guidelines.html, accessed 2 September 2009; Invista "Lycra – Trademark Protection Campaign" http://www.lycra.com/g_en/webpage.aspx?id=181, accessed 2 September 2009.

61 R. Folsom and L. Teply, *Trademarked Generic Words*, 89 Yale Law Journal 1323, 1354 (1980); Ingerl and Rohnke (*supra* note 5), at § 49 marginal note 35.

62 Folsom and Teply (*supra* note 61), at p. 1354.

E. Conclusion

This presentation has shown that a number of questions connected to the defences of non-use and genericness have received a new twist through the case law of the ECJ. Whereas genericness was once judged from a trader's perspective it has shifted towards a consumer perspective. Whereas it was once debated whether a objective approach, which includes sales for the sole purpose of upholding the trade mark, or a subjective approach, which excludes such use but includes honest *de minimis* use, should be taken in assessing non-use, the ECJ found in favour of the latter approach.

These changes or clarifications in the case law do have a substantial practical impact on how trade mark proprietors have to take care of their registered signs. Before the harmonization of European trade mark law it might have been sufficient to make sure that traders and distributors do not use a specific trade mark as a generic term. Now the attention has shifted onto the consumer. *Ex curia* actions, such as Google Inc.'s against the publishers of dictionaries concerning the use of the verb *(to) google*, are one of many ways to make sure that a trade mark stays a distinctive term in the mind of the consumer. From a legal perspective such actions are necessary and understandable, but they are often perceived as hostile and over-zealous by the general public. Then again with regards to non-use the case law of the ECJ has also provided some facilitation for trade mark owners in allowing them to proof genuine use by using their mark only for after-sales activities or only to a very limited extent.

Defences in Patent Litigation: When can a Patent be unenforceable? (Polish and German Perspective)

Justyna Ożegalska-Trybalska

I. Introduction

The patent is arguably a powerful weapon giving the patent holder an intellectual property right to exclude others from making, using and selling the patented invention. In practice, however, when a patentee wants to enforce his rights he might face a number of situation in which his patent would be unenforceable or his patent claim would not be permitted under the patent law.

Apart from a brief presentation of possible defences in a patent litigation in various countries, this article analyses in more detail two typical situations when a patent cannot be successfully enforced due to a lack of infringement. The situation takes place, first, when the allegedly infringing act falls outside the scope of the patent claim, and, second, when the patentee enforces his right against an alleged infringer, and subsequently the patent is found to be invalid.

Even though the European patent case law refers to many examples of an unsuccessful patent enforcement because a lack of infringement or invalidity, there are no unified standards used by national courts in this regard.[1] This article discusses the problem more closely from the perspective of the Polish and German law and practice.

II. Procedural and substantial defences in a patent infringement proceeding – general remarks

Generally speaking, in a patent litigation proceeding, the alleged infringer has two kinds of legal grounds to attack the patent holder: procedural defences and substantial defences. Traditionally, among procedural defences are the lack of jurisdiction, *res judicata,* a prior court action based on different patent but covering the same product.

1 More on significant differences in legislation and case law in the context of 'wrongful' patent enforcement: Ch. Heath, *Wrongful Patent Enforcement – Threats and Post-Infringement Invalidity in Comparative Perspective,* 39 IIC 307 (2008).

There are also specific procedural defences developed in European patent law, such for example the so-called 'torpedo' action. The action, also known as 'Italian Torpedo' or 'Belgian Torpedo' enjoyed rising attention among practitioners as a defence strategy against potential patent infringement mainly in cross-border patent litigation in Europe.[2] The action is also used in Germany,[3] but there are no notified examples of use of such a patent defence by the defendants in Polish patent litigations. The idea of the action is that filling a petition for declaratory judgements of non infringement by a potential infringer can block actions by the patentee in countries where an infringement action is expected since, according to Art. 21 of the Council Regulation (EC) No. 44/2001 of 22 December 2000 on jurisdiction and the recognition and enforcement of judgments in civil and commercial matters,[4] such a claim cannot be heard until the declaration of non-infringement is resolved.

Even though defending itself on the procedural ground could be a quick and effective way of terminating allegation, this kind of patent defence is available only in limited cases. Thus, in patent litigation, most often the substantial defences are used by defendants based on the arguments that the accused activity does not infringe a patent or the patent is invalid. Next to the above-mentioned universal substantial defences, there are also a number of country-specific defences.

For example, under the so-called 'inequitable conduct defence' developed under the US patent case law, during patent litigation the defendant can present evidence that the patentee was devious in getting the patent. If it proves that the patentee intentionally misled the patent office about material information, the patent will not be enforceable.[5] In U.S practice also co-called prosecution history estoppels (or file wrapper estoppels) is widely used which implies that the patentee cannot claim protection for what he has disclaimed during patent examination process. So, proving that at the stage of patent examination the patent owner has excluded some solution from the scope of the patent, could also make the patent enforceable.[6]

2 R. Schuster, C. Rübel: *Germany: Why Torpedos have backfired,* Managing Intellectual Property, July/August 2003, p. 98-100.

3 For interesting developments of German case law affecting the reasoning for instigating 'torpedo action' see Düsseldorf District Court, 2000 GRUR 692 – *NMR-Kontrastmittel* and the later decision of Hamburg District Court, 2002 GRUR Int. 1025 – *Seifenverpackung.*

4 *OJ EC L 012 of 16 January 2001, p. 1.*

5 *J.P.Stevens & Co. V. Lex Tex Ltd.* 747 F. 2 d 1553 223 U.S.P.T.O 1089 (Fed.Cir. 1984).

6 See: *Warner Jenkinson Co. Inc. v. Hilton Davis Chemical* Co. (117 S. Ct. 1040 41 (U.S. P.Q) 2d 1865 (1997), *Wilson Sporting Goods Co. v. David Geoffrey & Associates*, 904 F.2d 677 (Fed. Cir. 1990).

This defence is used in the US as the main defence against action for not infringement under the doctrine of equivalents and, exceptionally, in some countries in Europe.[7] Under the Polish patent law, the documents provided and statements made during the examination stage rule have no legal importance in infringement litigation. As a principle, also in Germany there is no practice of construction of patent claims on the basis of prosecution files.[8]

Under another defence, known in the UK as the 'Gillette Defence'[9] and in Germany as 'Formstein Defence'[10], the defendant can argue that the patent cannot be infringed since his allegedly infringing activity is old or obvious relative to what is claimed in the patent.[11]

Next to the above, national patent regulations usually provide a list of situations which are not considered as patent infringements. The list of such limitations is provided by Art. 69 of the Polish Industrial Property Code, and Sec. 11 of the German Patent Law. One of such situations often used as a way of rejecting patent infringement claim is employing of an invention for research and experimental purposes, for the evaluation thereof, analysis or teaching. This so-called "research exemption" or "safe harbour exemption" is recognised in many countries and its scope is widely discussed in national jurisdictions,[12] mainly in the context of pharmaceutical patents.

According to the interpretation of Polish courts, the 'research exemption' applies to situations when the patented invention is used as a research tool in scientific, research, experimental, analytical and didactic activities, and the activity involving patented invention is not aimed at achieving results which can be commercialised.[13] In Germany, the scope of this exemption is not entirely clear.[14] It seems however that the German courts understands the exemption more broadly in the way that the research exemption covers scientific, research as well as research for commercial proposes, as far as tests are intended yield

7 For example, see decision of Dutch High Court of 13 January 1995, 28 IIC 748 (1997) – *Ciba Geigy AG v. Oté Optics B.V.* , where the court confirmed that history of the procedure of granting patent can be helpful in the assessment of disputed features of the patent.

8 See BGH of 12 March 2002, 34 IIC 302 (2003) – *Plastic Pipe (Kunststoffrohrteil).*

9 (1913) 30 RPC 465 – *Gillette Safe Razor Co. v. Anglo American Trading Co Ltd.*

10 BGH 18 IIC 795 (1987) – *Molded Curbstone (Formstein).*

11 J. Pagenberg, *Interpretation of Patent Claims – Influence of Prior Art and the Knowledge of the Skilled Person for the Scope of Protection*, 2002 High Technology Protection Summit, paper, available at CASRIP Symposium Series No. 8 (2003), p. 9, under http://www.law.washington.edu/casrip/symposium/Number8/.

12 More on European approach on experimental research see more: W. R. Cornish, *Experimental Use of Patented Inventions in European Community States*, 29 IIC 735 (1998).

13 Supreme Administration Court of 5 May 2007, Case II GSK 92/07, LexPolonica No. 388201.

14 See A. van der Merwe, *Experimental Use and Submission of Data for Regulatory Approval*, 31 IIC 380 (2000); W. R. Cornish (*supra* note 12), p. 735-753.

knowledge on the patent subject matter including its use that are intended to remove an existing uncertainty.[15]

1. Non infringement defence

In case of a patent litigation, an obvious way of defending oneself against a patent infringement action is to argue that the scope of the patent does not cover an allegedly infringing activity, or the patent is not broad enough to cover infringing features. The court must take this argument into consideration by making an assessment of the scope of the patent.

Traditionally, the scope of a patent, that the area covered by an exclusivity arising from the patent, is determined by patent claims included in a patent application. The aim of an interpretation of patent claims is to identify the subject of an invention and to determine the area covered by the patent. So, the content of patent claims has a fundamental importance at the stage of the examination of a patent application when the patentability of an invention is examined, as well as at the stage of the patent enforcement, when a litigation court determines the scope of a patentee's exclusivity over the invention.

Defining the extend of patent protection in a patent infringement litigation is a matter of interpreting a particular patent claims in suit and always begs the question whether to apply general rules of the interpretation to each particular case. The success of patent enforcement depends on the determination of the scope of the patent, thus, to a large extend, on how patent claims are interpreted by a court.

The general legal basis for determination of the scope of the patents in Europe is Art. 69 of the European Patent Convention (EPC) under which extent of the protection conferred by a European patent is determined by the terms of the claims and the description and drawings should support interpretation of the claims.

The identical use of the wording of the patent claim features by an alleged patent infringer which constitutes the literal patent infringement does not poses a problem for the party enforcing the patent. The scope of the patent protection, however, is not strictly limited by the language of the claim, but may extend beyond its linguistic meaning. In cases when the features of a protected invention are not accomplished by an allegedly infringing solution in the identical way, the application of the so-called doctrine of equivalence is necessary.

15 BGH (1997) RPC 623 = 28 IIC 103 (1997) – *Clinical Tests I (Klinische Versuche I)* and (1998) RPC 423 – *Clinical Tests II (Klinische Versuche II)*.

For many years, the doctrine was widely applied by courts as an instrument for protecting patents beyond the claim language.[16] Now, both the European case law as well as the provisions of the EPC, and especially the current wording of the special Protocol of Interpretation to Art. 69 of EPC (as amended by EPC 2000),[17] make it clear that under the European patent law the broad interpretation of patent claims is permitted, which allows to extend the scope of the patent also for equivalents of the elements indicated in the claims.[18] Generally speaking, the technical means are equivalent if they are used for the same purpose, have the same technical functions, and help in achieving the same technical effect.[19]

Most national patent laws in Europe, including Sec. 14 of the German Patent Law, repeat the rules of determination of a patent scope provided by Art. 69 of EPC and the Protocol of Interpretation. Nonetheless, as a practice shows, even when applying the same regulation, the result of claim interpretation and thus of the scope of the patent (and the success of patent enforcement) can be different,

16 A. Stenvik: *Protection for Equivalents Under the Patent Law – Theories and Practice,* 32 IIC 3 (2001).

17 The new text of the Protocol adopted by the Administrative Council of the European Patent Organization in its decision of 28 June 2001 (see OJ EPO 2001, Special edition No. 4, p. 55) has become an integral part of the Revision Act of 29 November 2000 under Art. 3 (2), second sentence, of that Act. It should be underlined that added by EPC 2000 new Sec. 2 of Interpretation Protocol to Art. 69 of the EPC, 'formalizing' equivalents does not change interpretation rules used before it come into the force. In the light of practice to date, this provision should be treated only as a formal explanation and reminder for the courts that equivalents are covered by the scope of the European patent so far as they can be interpreted out of the content of patent claims.

18 According to Art. 1 of the Protocol on the Interpretation of Art. 69 EPC as revised by the Act revising the EPC of 29 November 2000, "*Art. 69 should not be interpreted as meaning that the extent of the protection conferred by a European patent is to be understood as that defined by the strict, literal meaning of the wording used in the claims, the description and drawings being employed only for the purpose of resolving an ambiguity found in the claims. Nor should it be taken to mean that the claims serve only as a guideline and that the actual protection conferred may extend to what, from a consideration of the description and drawings by a person skilled in the art, the patent proprietor has contemplated. On the contrary, it is to be interpreted as defining a position between these extremes which combines a fair protection for the patent proprietor with a reasonable degree of legal certainty for third parties*". The Art. 2 of the Protocol specifies that "*for the purpose of determining the extent of protection conferred by a European patent, due account shall be taken of any element which is equivalent to an element specified in the claims*".

19 Generally speaking, in order to answer the question whether a technical solution which is not an exact imitation of a claimed features is covered by the patent, the European courts developed the following, three-stages test: basically the same function – basically the same way of accomplishment – basically the same result. J. Pagenberg, *Conclusion and Proposals for Greater Harmonization,* in: J. Pagenberg / W. R. Cornish (eds.), *Interpretation of Patents in Europe. Application of Art. 69 EPC*, p. 259 (Munich 2006).

since in practice it is highly influenced by the national tradition of claim interpretation and the understanding of the concept of protection against equivalents, as well as the technical knowledge of judges involved in particular patent infringement proceedings.

Germany is one of the countries in Europe in which the special methods of patent claims interpretation have been developed. The traditional test used by the German courts consists of the following prerequisites of equivalence: (1) the allegedly infringing embodiment has the same technical effect, (2) the allegedly infringing solution could be derived by a skilled person from the disclosure of the patent claims, (3) the allegedly equivalent solution does not belong to the prior art and would have been patentable over prior art.[20]

A liberal (broad) interpretation of patent claims confirmed by the German courts in many decisions on patent infringement is traditionally opposed to a strict English patent claims construction. The main difference between the methods of patent claim interpretation used in Germany and the UK results in divergences in the assessment of patent infringement, comes from a different way of reading patent claims by the person skilled in the art.[21] While, according to German approach the assessment of equivalent features should be made independently from patent claims,[22] in the light of the English test such an assessment must be focused exactly on claims.[23] As a consequence, under the English patent law, features which in fact are functional equivalents, but are not expressed in the patent claims are considered outside of the patent scope.[24] It should be noted that recently the tendency is observed in the German patent case law to change the previous approach and to interpret patent claims on the basis of the semantic context of them, which is considered as a step toward the elimination of differences with the English practice.

In the Polish case law regarding patent infringement, relatively poor compared to other courtiers, the theory of equivalence has not been developed in the con-

20 The above test has been determined by the BGH in the landmark *Formstein* decision (*supra* note 10).

21 See for more: W. Cornish, *Scope and Interpretation of Patent claims under Art. 69 of the European Patent Convention*, in: H.C. Hansen (ed.), *International Intellectual Property Law & Policy*, p. 34-3 – 34-10 (2000).

22 German approach developed in *Formstein* decision (*supra* note 10).

23 English courts apply the test of the questions initially defined in *Catnic Components Ltd. v. Hill and Smith Ltd.*, (1982) RPC 183 (H.L. 1980), and then modified in cases: *Improver Corporation v. Remington* [1990] F.S.R. 181, 189 and *Kirin-Amgen v. Hoechst Marion Roussel* (2004) UKHL 46.

24 See R. Hacon, J. Pagenberg, *Concise European Patent Law*, p. 79 (Hague 2005).

text of patent infringement litigation.[25] In the absence of court decisions determining rules for interpretation of patent claims, Art. 63 Sec. 2 of the Polish Industrial Property Code[26] is a starting point for the determination of the scope of a patent and its possible extension to equivalents of the claimed features. It stipulates that *"the scope of the protection sought shall be determined by the claims contained in the patent specification. The patent specification and drawings may be used to interpret the claims*". Although it seems to be consistent with Art. 69 of the EPC, there is a slight but important difference between the two. According to Art. 69 of the EPC, the description and drawings *are to be used* to interpret the claims, while under the Polish Industrial Property Code they *may be used* for such an interpretation.

The interpretation of the different wording of these provisions may have a practical consequence for the determination of the scope of the patents enforced in Poland.

First, it is not possible to argue that, because of the identity of the Polish provision and Art. 69 of the EPC, by way of analogy, the broad interpretation of claims of national patents and the application of the theory of equivalence is allowed. Second, the literal interpretation of the Polish provision does not allow for the interpretation of a patent claim out of its language, if the meaning of a patent claim of a national patent is clear. In such a case, according to the *clara non sunt interpretanda* rule, there is no ground for extending the interpretation for a description and drawings and the scope of the patent should be determined exclusively by the patent claims. The description and drawings can be taken into consideration only if the claims are not clear.[27] Thus, when patent claims are clear, extending the scope of a national patent for features contained in the description that includes equivalences but not covered by the patent claims is not allowed. Even in cases where, due to unclear wording of patent claims, the determination of the scope of a patent is supported by the description and drawing, their content should limit the scope of the patent protection.

The literal interpretation of the above provision of the Polish patent law leads to the conclusion that there is no formal ground for the courts to extend the scope of the national patents out of the scope of patent claim and the description. Moreover, the direct reference to the Protocol of Interpretation to Art. 69 of EPC is not possible, which clearly recognises protection by equivalents, since it applies to European and not to national patents.

25 In practice the equivalence theory is used by the Polish Patent Office in the examination proceeding as well as the patent invalidation proceeding; see, for example, Board of Appeal at the Polish Patent Office of 26 September 1976, Case No. 1459/76.

26 OJ from 2003, No. 119, Sec. 1117 (unified version).

27 M. du Vall: *Prawo patentowe*, p. 250-251 (Warsaw 2008).

Clearly, such a situation creates a dualism in regard to the determination of the extent of a patent protecting an invention in Poland. One hand, there is no doubt that, due to a priority of an international agreement over the national law, in Poland European patents must enjoy an extended protection guaranteed by the EPC and the Protocol of Interpretation.[28] On the other hand, there is no formal ground for using the same standards of interpretation to national patents granted by the Polish Patent Office. From the point of view of patent holders it means that in case of an infringement by equivalence in Poland it could be more difficult to enforce a European patent than a patent granted on the basis of the provisions of the national patent law provisions.

2. Patent invalidity defence

Next to the non-infringement defence, another commonly used in the patent infringement litigation is the defendant's statement that the enforced patent is invalid. The idea behind this defence is simple: the patent can be enforced (patent litigation is justified) only if the patent really belongs to the claimant. If the patent is invalid, there are no grounds for the claimant to claim infringement of his rights. Since questioning the patent validity is the most obvious defence against an alleged patent infringement, the patent holder should carefully consider the advantages of patent enforcement and the risk of losing the patent.

Grounds for such an invalidation action are usually the lack of patentability requirements, namely the lack of novelty or inventiveness. Under most jurisdictions, this objection is, however, not directly investigated and formally confirmed by the court carrying out an infringement litigation, but by some other body – usually a patent office or a special patent court – in the independent invalidation proceeding.

Unlike in countries like Holland, Italy or Switzerland, in Poland and Germany infringement and invalidation proceedings are separated. Moreover, in contrast to Germany, in Poland there are no specialized patent court(s) or a patent court division responsible for patent infringement cases.

In Poland, patent infringement proceedings are carried out before the common district courts according to the procedure for commercial matters (Art. 479 (1)-(27) of the Code of Civil Procedure) while the exclusive jurisdiction over invalidation of patents belongs to the Polish Patent Office. The invalidation procedure is governed by Arts. 255-258 of the Industrial Property Code and the provisions

28 It should be noted that there is a collision between provisions of EPC and the provision.

of the Code of Administrative Procedure (excluding provisions of time limits for issuing a decision).

The legal basis for patent invalidation in Poland is Art. 89 of the Polish Industrial Property Code, according to which "a patent may be declared invalid in whole or in part at the request of any person having a legitimate interest therein, who is able to prove that the statutory requirements for the grant of a patent have not been satisfied". As confirmed by the legal doctrine and the case law, under the above mentioned provision the defendant in infringement proceeding is considered eligible for initiating invalidation proceeding.

Similarly to Poland, in Germany there is a strict separation of infringement proceedings and invalidation proceedings. Infringement actions are dealt with specialised higher regional courts, especially those in Düsseldorf (District Court and Court of Appeal), Mannheim and Munich. Invalidity proceedings are handled by the Federal Patent Court in Munich under Sec. 81 of the German Patent Act. For both infringement and invalidity proceeding the last instance is the Federal Court of Justice.

Since during the infringement actions the litigation court cannot decide on a validity of a patent, the alleged patent infringer cannot formally defend himself against the patent infringement with a counterclaim based on an invalidity of the enforced patent. In an infringement suit, a litigation court is not authorised to evaluate the patent validity, which can be assessed by the responsible body (The Patent Office in Poland, The Federal Patent Court in Germany) in a separate invalidation proceeding under a separate request for declaration of patent invalidity.

While considering the consequences of separation of infringement and invalidation proceedings in the context of patent enforceability, the number of important questions raised. First, should the court suspend the infringement proceeding until a decision on patent validity is issued or continue infringement proceeding and resolve the dispute without consideration of validity of the enforced patent? Second, should the court of a patent litigation be bounded by a decision invalidating patent if such a decision is issued before the infringement case is resolved? Third, what is a legal effect of a decision invalidating patent? Fourth, should the decision on patent invalidation allow for reopening of past infringement proceedings? If so, should it result in the restitution of damages awards and courts costs incurred in the infringement suit?

The national regulations and practice in this regard differ one from another. For example, according to Art. 177 § 1 Sec. 3 of the Polish Code for the Civil Procedure a court *might* suspend a proceeding if the resolution of the case depends on the prior decision of a public administrative body, which means that there is no formal obligation to suspend the patent infringement proceeding if an invalidity proceeding is raised. As interpreted by the Polish Supreme Court, the possibility for a court to suspend the proceeding "*does not mean freedom in taking the decision, but an obligation to consider and balance all circumstances justified by the particular case*".[29]

Despite the above directive, in practice it rarely happens that the court suspends the infringement proceeding when a defendant files the request for invalidation of an formally granted an industrial property right to the Polish Patent Office. Moreover, in such cases no justification or a very unclear justification is given by the court for not suspending the infringement proceeding.

Thus no assessment would possibly be made by the Polish courts in regard to of how likely the patent is to be invalidated. By contrast, in Germany, after the defendant has filed its invalidation action at the German Federal Patent Court, the court of litigation has the possibility to suspend the litigation procedure until the invalidation procedure has been finalised. The suspension of the procedure depends on the litigation court's opinion regarding the most probable outcome.[30] In the case of German patents, the decision on suspension of the patent litigation is made if the allegedly infringed patent has been granted without any opposition procedure. If the patent was already subject of a review during an opposition procedure or an appeal opposition procedure the German Federal Patent Courts usually do not suspend the litigation.

Compared to Poland, the German practice in this regard seems to be more appropriate. The question whether the plaintiff enforces a valid patent is crucial for the assessment of the patent infringement. If the patent is invalid (was invalid at the time of the alleged infringement), there is (was) no exclusive right preventing others from using the patented invention. In that context an important problem is raised: what is the relevant moment from which a patent should be considered invalid – the date of the issue of the patent invalidation decision or the date of granting the patent? In other words, the question is what the legal effect of the decision issued in invalidation proceeding is and how it impacts infringement proceeding. Does the decision take effect *ex tunc* or *ex nunc*?

Since the patent invalidation decision declares that the patent should be never granted, the logical answer should be that this confirms the *ex tunc* (retroactive) effect of such a decision, and so the effect of the decision from the date of grating the patent. Accordingly, when the patent is invalidated during patent infringement action, the court should not ignore it since, if there is no patent, there is no patent infringement and the plea should be dismissed.

29 Polish Supreme Court of 10 June 2002, Case II CKN 826/00.

30 Ch. W. Appelt, H. Goddar: *Enforcement of Patents in Europe – Germany as an Example,* accompanying paper to the lectures at Innovation Support Training programmes (ISTP), Prague, 27 November 2006, available at: http://www.ip4inno.eu/index.php?id=187.

Even though such an approach seems to be justifiable, the recent Polish case law dealing with the question of the relation between industrial property right infringement dispute and invalidation proceeding does not confirm it. In the decision of 6 January 2009,[31] regarding the infringement of the right to a registered design, the Polish Supreme Court states that in "the proceeding in which the plaintiff proves that is an owner of the right to the design, a possible decision invalidating that right, incidentally having *ex nunc* effect, has no prejudicial importance". As a result, the Polish Supreme Court stated that the plaintiff's claim to suspend infringement proceeding in the case of invalidation proceeding was unjustified. The starting point for such a conclusion was the reasoning of the courts that Art. 177 § 1 Sec. 3 of the Polish Code for the Civil Procedure allows suspension of the court proceeding if the resolution of the case depends of the former administrative decision content of which is an essential element of the legal basis for substantial or procedural resolution of the case. Since in the court's view there is no connection between the decision issued in the proceeding of a design right invalidation and the court proceeding in which the owner of an intellectual property right enforces it – there is no obligation for the court to suspend the later once invalidation procedure is initiated.

Even if indeed there is no formal connection between infringement and invalidation proceedings, the above court's approach ignoring a practical consequences of declaring patent infringement before the decision on validity of patent is issued should be criticised. In practice, the declaration of the *ex nunc* effect of the decision means that there is no possibility for a patent infringer to reopen a patent infringement proceeding and even after the invalidation of the patent the infringer would be prevented from doing what everybody else could do.[32]

A different approach seems to be present in the German case law dealing with the question of a legal effect of the decision invalidating patent and its impact on a decision issued in a patent infringement proceeding.

As ruled by the Düsseldorf Court of Appeal in the *Restitutionsklage III* case[33] of 2006, there is a causal connection between the court decision on infringement based on the assumption of the patent's validity and the later decision of the Federal Supreme Court on the invalidation of the patent because invalidation of the patent takes effect from the date of grant. As acknowledged by the court, the final decision that finds patent infringement can be set aside where the patent has been revoked after the infringement decision has become final. The decision was based, by way of analogy, on Sec. 580 (6) of the German Code of Civil Procedure under which "*the decision of an ordinary or a former extraordinary court*

31 Polish Supreme Court of 16 January 2009, Case VCKS 241/08, LexPolonica No. 484688.

32 Ch. Heath (*supra* note 1), p. 318.

33 Düsseldorf Court of Appeal of 11 May 2006, Case 2 U 86/05, 39 IIC 355 (2008).

or an administrative court, on which a [currant] decision [at issue] is based, is set aside by way of a final decision". In the court's opinion, even though a patent is ordinarily granted by an act of an administrative body rather than the "decision of an ordinary court", the analogy with the mentioned provision is justified. In the court's reasoning, once the patent that the infringement court had to regard as valid is subsequently invalidated, the legal basis of the previous decision on finding for patent infringement has been undermined to the same extent as the decision that was based on a previous judicial decision.

In the *Spundfass II* case[34] of 2007, the Düsseldorf Court of Appeal confirmed that a patent invalidation decision may be a ground for setting aside a previous final decision on infringement but only if the patent at issue is invalidated completely or partially, or formally limited in scope by the amendments of the patent claims or the description.[35]

The approach taken by the German courts suggest that in the systems with split infringement and invalidity proceedings, the retrial can be available. The German law also clearly recognizes the consequences of retrial, such as the reimbursement of costs already incurred (costs of the court and of the representatives in the infringement proceeding paid by the alleged infringer)[36] as well as reimbursement of payments made by the alleged infringer as a unjust enrichment of the patentee.[37]

3. Determination of the scope of the patent during granting procedure and patent litigation

Considering the problem of the scope of the patent in the context of the "scope of its enforceability", the question arose whether courts resolving disputes on patent infringement and making assessment of the scope of the patent may (or should) be supported by the patent office that granted the allegedly infringed patent.

Although no common practice in this regard is developed so far, there is a legal framework for cooperation between the body that decides if a patent can be successfully enforced and the body that issued an allegedly infringed patent. This is mainly practiced in the US under the so-called *primary jurisdiction doctrine*,

34 Düsseldorf Court of Appeal of 9 August 2007, Case 2 U 49/06, 39 IIC 357 (2008).

35 As the court observed, "the principle of *res judicata* that applies to the final decision should only be overridden in case when the legal basis of the previous decision have been formally repealed". Limitation of the scope of the patent by a patentee in oral invalidation proceeding in order to avoid invalidation could not be linked with its revocation and cannot be a ground for applying Sec. 580 (6) of the German Code of Civil Procedure.

36 Düsseldorf Court of Appeal (*supra* note 33).

37 Ch. Heath (*supra* note 1), p. 320.

allowing courts to enjoy administrative assistance of a patent office in the interpretation of a patent claim.[38] Also Art. 25 of the EPC allows national courts involved in patent infringement or invalidation litigation to get a technical opinion on the European patent. The possible practical function of this provision is, however, limited by secondary regulation to the EPC that requires the national courts to ask the question by distinguishing the technical and the legal aspects. So, formally the European Patent Office is not allowed to issue a technical opinion on the scope of the patent, but it could still be a front door for a court of litigation assessing the scope of the patent in the context of infringement to check how the European Patent Office understands the scope of monopoly claimed by the patentee at the stage of patent grating. In contrast to the Germany, where a legal ground for a court to use 'administrative interpretation of patent claims' in some situations could be Sec. 29 of the German Patent Law,[39] there is no legal mechanism like this in Poland.

III. Conclusions

As practice shows, it is not easy to get a patent, but it is even harder sometimes to enforce it. The decision to grant a patent does not provide full legal certainty over its factual validity and, thus, its enforceability. The later is often unverified until after the patent litigation proceeding is started by the patentee.

The formal dualism of patent infringement and invalidation proceedings in many countries, as well as the national court practice in regard to the prejudicial effect of patent invalidation proceeding, have a direct influence on the success of patent enforcement (and – at the same time – the success of raising an invalidity claim in a patent infringement litigation).

Strict separation of the infringement and invalidation proceedings and independency between decision of infringement and decision of invalidity creates legal uncertainty for a patent holder, but also an alleged patent infringer. Even a long time after the infringement dispute is resolved and the court has confirmed that patent infringement has occurred, such a decision can be negatively influenced by the decision issued in an invalidation proceeding if patent invalidity is declared. Even if the defendant raises an invalidity claim and initiates a separate invalidation proceeding, he can still be targeted for patent infringement even if

38 U.S. Supreme Court 352 U.S. 59 (1956) – *United States v. Western Pacific Railroad Co.*

39 According to Sec. 29 (1) of German Patent Law "*the Patent Office shall be required to give opinions at the requests of the courts or State Prosecutor's Office on the questions affecting patents if divergent expert opinions are submitted in the proceeding*".

there is a high probability that the allegedly infringed patent will be confirmed to be invalid.

From the point of view of the patent holder, legal uncertainty in regard to his patent enforceability is even greater since the same body that confirmed patentability of his invention at the stage of granting a patent finds its non-patentability at the stage of patent invalidation.

The legal uncertainty could be eliminated in different ways, such for example the creation of a specialized national patent court (courts) responsible for infringement and invalidation litigation.[40]

In countries such Poland and Germany, where the separation is maintained, there should be legal rules introduced clarifying an obligation for the courts to suspend the infringement litigation proceeding when formal patent invalidity claim is raised. The 'quality' of a patent ensuring high probability of successful patent enforcement could be achieved by the adoption of mutual rules for determining scope of the patent used by the national patent office and courts.

In order to ensure unified patent enforceability in Europe, clear and uniform standards should be worked out in regard to the interpretation of patent claims. So far, the determination of the scope of the patent and thus success of patent enforcement has been influenced by the national concept of the 'legal nature' of patent claims and the method used by national courts for the interpretation of patent claims.

In countries like Poland, where the rules for determining the scope of national patents differ from those applied to European patents, the necessary amendments of the patent law should be introduced according to Art. 69 of the EPC and the Protocol of Interpretation. Until it happens, the possible solution for eliminating the existing dualism in regard to patent claims interpretation is to allow for a broad interpretation of patent claims but only within the scope determined by the content of patent claims. This could be justified only, if the Polish courts would follow the English approach according to which the Protocol of Interpretation to Art. 69 of the EPC does not allow for an interpretation of European patents beyond the scope of patent claims.[41]

40 M. du Vall, Analiza aspektów gospodarczych i warunków prawno-organizacyjnych oraz społecznych w zakresie rozwiązań dotyczących utworzenia sądu własności przemysłowej, report prepared for the Polish Ministry of Economy, Crakow, May 2007, published under: http://www.mg.gov.pl/NR/rdonlyres/490197EB-3AB4-4800-9749-256E837C5FFE/39113/analiza.pdf.

41 M. du Vall (*supra* note 27), p. 240.

Dualism in German Patent Law and its Implications for Patent Litigation

Sven Hetmank

1. Introduction

In contrast to Polish Patent Law and to Patent Law of almost every other country, German Patent Law is characterized by a separation of powers between judicial and administrative branches. There are two consequences: First, there are two separate court systems and procedures for administrative and civil law issues side by side: The Patent Revocation Procedures including opposition, nullity and compulsory licence proceedings – under exclusive jurisdiction of the Patent Office and the Federal Patent Court and a separate patent infringement proceeding under jurisdiction of the civil courts. Second, because of this separation the court in patent infringement litigation is bound by the decision of the Patent Office to grant the patent and in turn the judicial examination of a legally granted patent is not within the jurisdiction of the infringement court.[1]

Such a separation, however, can lead to some very serious implications which may give rise to call the doctrine of dualism into question.

I will focus on four examples of such implications: The objection of invalidity in German infringement proceedings and the "Formstein objection" (2. and 3.), a separate patent as a defence in infringement proceedings (4.), the revocation after a final and non-appealable judgement in the infringement proceedings (5.) and a patent claim which is irreproducible and incomprehensible (6.).

In conclusion I will ask the following questions: Does the Doctrine of Dualism lead to an over-enforcement and is the Doctrine of Dualism worth to keep or is it even a worthwhile model for other countries and the European Patent System?

2. Objection of Invalidity

Is it possible to raise the objection of invalidity in German Patent Litigation? Of cause the answer is "No" - because this would at the same time call into question

1 Cf. R. Kraßer, *Patentrecht*, 6th ed. (2009), p. 735 et seq.

the binding act of the grant of the patent. As long as a patent is formally effective, the infringement court has no competence to examine the patent, is strictly bound by it and has to accept the patent as it was granted.[2] Especially a lack of inventiveness or a lack of novelty is completely irrelevant in infringement proceedings.

Instead the defendant who wants to plead the invalidity of a patent in infringement proceedings has to file an opposition with the Patent Office or an invalidation action with the *German Federal Patent Court.* And doing so, such a pending opposition or invalidation action enables the defendant to ask for stay of proceedings according to Sec. 148 of the German Code of Civil Procedure. Sec. 148 reads as follows:

> "The court may, if the decision of the case depends wholly or partly on the existence or non-existence of a legal relationship forming the subject of another pending action or is to be determined by an administrative authority, direct that the proceedings be suspended until the other action or a decision is settled."

However, this means that the court indirectly has to examine the validity of the patent, because the infringement court has to examine the prospects of success of the invalidation action.[3]

Referring this to students or colleagues, it is hard to find understanding and acceptance. By wearing a deep frown they wonder if that is not inconsequent and they ask: Is it not a doubling of work load, because the same question of validity is examined by two different courts in two different procedures?[4] Furthermore one could ask whether such a restriction in defending is not a little bit too disadvantageous for the defendant and wouldn't this be an overprotection in favour of the patent owner.

At least it has to be mentioned that German courts quite rarely granting the stay of an infringement case due to this provision.[5] Usually the stay is only granted if the invalidation action or the opposition is very likely and obviously successful[6] and everyone who has to deal with patent law cases knows only too well, that cases in patent law are rarely predictable or at least appreciable.

2 P. Mes in: W. Prinz zu Waldeck und Pyrmont, J. Drexl, M.J. Adelmann, R. Brauneis, R. Nack (eds.), *Patents and Technological Progress in a Globalized World. Liber Amicorum Straus*, p. 401, 405 (Berlin 2009).

3 Zöller, *ZPO*, 27th ed. (2009), § 148, marginal notes 5 et seq.; R. Kraßer (*supra* note 1), p. 890 et seq.

4 See P. Mes (*supra* note 2), at p. 407.

5 See P. Mes (*supra* note 2), at p. 406.

6 See P. Mes (*supra* note 2), at p. 406 et seq.; BGH 1987 GRUR 284 – *Transport Vehicle (Transportfahrzeug)*.

3. "Formstein" objection

When it comes to the so called "Formstein" objection, frown lines of students and colleagues are often getting even deeper.

In a decision from 1986 the *German Federal Court of Justice* created a new defence for an alleged infringer, who uses a solution which has been developed from the prior art.[7] In this case the plaintiff was the owner of a German patent filed in 1979. Claims 1 and 2 read as follows:

> "1. Integral or cross-sectionally multi-part moulded stone with a longitudinal trough for dewatering lines at the side of the road, characterised by the fact that it comprises at least one cross channel branching off from the longitudinal trough and opening into the side of the stone facing away from the street center.
>
> 2. Moulded stone in accordance with Claim 1, characterized by the fact that the cross channel has a small inclination."

The disadvantages of the prior art as set out in the description are that usually a larger rainwater sewerage is necessary because the entire rainwater accumulating on the surface of the street has to be drained off and that accumulated dirt and mud can get into the rainwater sewerage. Therefore the alleged advantage of the invention is that very large quantities of rainwater can be drained from the surface of the street and dirt and mud will not get into the sewerage due to the cross channels which are branching off from the longitudinal channel. To some extent one could say that this is a rather simple kind of a roadside drainage – using effects which may have been known since ancient times.

Of course the inevitable happened: The defendant city council was building a street with a surface of collecting paving stones. On the sides of those streets there was a row of common and conventional curbstones with small gaps in those rows to make the rainwater seeping into a layer of gravel next to the street. Although the effect of the drainage was the same as provided by the patented invention the defendant city did not use specially moulded and customized curbstones with an integrated longitudinal trough and therefore did not use curbstones in accordance with the literally teaching of the patent at issue. This means there was no use of the teachings of the patent under a literal interpretation of the patent claims. So the further question arose: Is there an equivalent use of the patent at issue?

Under the so called doctrine of equivalents, there may be infringement even if the accused act or product falls outside the meaning of the words of the claim. There are three requirements to be fulfilled:[8] First, the modified element per-

7 BGH 1986 GRUR 803= 18 IIC 795 (1987) – *Moulded Curbstone* (*Formstein*).

8 J. Pagenberg, R. Schuster in R. Hacon, J. Pagenberg (eds.), *Concise Patent Law*, 2nd ed. (2008), Art. 69 EPC, marginal note 12; BGH 34 IIC 197 (2003) - *Custodiol II*.

forms substantially the same function and produces substantially the same result (Gleichwirkung). Second, it is obvious to a person skilled in the art on account of his technical knowledge, available to him at the priority date of the patent that the same result that is achieved by means of the element as expressed in the claim can be achieved by means of the modified element (Naheliegen). And third, a person skilled in the art would consider the modified claim feature as an equivalent to the feature in the claim (Gleichwertigkeit).

The *German Federal Court of Justice* did not answer the question of an equivalent use, but created a new defence for an alleged infringer. The court states:

> "The defence that the embodiment alleged to be an equivalent does not represent a patentable invention in view of the prior art is admissible. The defendant in patent infringement litigation can thus not only defend himself with the fact that the alleged patent infringing embodiment is known from the prior art, but also by the fact that it is obvious in view of the prior art."[9]

Such an objection does not call the patent as granted into question because the patent office did not examine the scope of protection in view of equivalent variants. The "Formstein-objection" therefore is limited to equivalent infringements and is not permitted in cases of literal infringement.[10] At the end of the day, however, once again one could ask, why the infringement court has to deal with the question of patentability while this is actually neither its task nor competence. And furthermore, why should there be a need for two separate court systems and two separate procedures, if the matter the courts are dealing with is essentially the same? Is this an adequate way to balance the interests of the defendant and the patent owner and to counteract "overenforcement"? And last but not least: Does this mean, that the scope of protection is to some extent restricted by the prior art? But if so, should we then not have a synchronized judgement of both the question of equivalence on the one side and the question of inventiveness on the other?[11]

One example may demonstrate how close the questions are to each other:[12]

> There is a prior art, characterized by the elements A, B, C, etc. and a patent, characterized by A, B and C'. Now the Patent Office (and in the revocation proceedings the Federal Patent Court) has to deal with the gap from A, B, C, to A, B, C' in order to find inventiveness or not. Now we have an infringing act which itself has been developed from the prior art using the elements A, B and C, which means that the infringement court has also to deal with the gap from A, B, C to A, B, C' in order to find infringement or not. In this case it

9 BGH *Moulded Curbstone* (*supra* note 7), at p. 800.

10 Cf. BGH 1997 GRUR 454 – *Kabeldurchführung* (regarding Utility Patent Law); R. Kraßer (*supra* note 1), p. 736 et seq.; Schulte, *Patentgesetz*, 8th ed. (2008), § 14 marginal note 78.

11 Cf. E. Popp, *Formstein-Einwand – reine Theorie?,* 2009 GRUR 318, 322.

12 For a further example see E. Popp (*supra* note 11), at p. 320.

might be difficult to see a distinction in judging the question whether there is an inventive step in the eye of a person skilled in the art and the question whether a person skilled in the art is able to identify the infringing act as having the same effect and as being equivalent to the patent at issue. Although these two questions are similar at the core of the matter, the criteria for answering these questions are different and may result into inconsistent court decisions and into a trap for the alleged infringer:[13] In the revocation proceedings, the court may consider the step from the prior art to the patent big enough in favour of inventiveness while the infringement court considers the almost identical step from the patent to the infringing variant not to be big enough in order to find for non-infringement. The alleged infringer in such a case may be prevented from using the pavement although in the view of one court the gap is big enough and in the view of the other court the same gap is not big enough. To avoid such inconsistency, equal criteria should be adopted in the finding of both: inventiveness and infringement at least insofar as the courts have to deal with the same prior art.[14]

Again it has to be mentioned, that the "Formstein-objection" is limited to equivalent infringement and is, in practice, of limited importance. In some cases, one could not help thinking that infringement courts are inclined to stretching the wording of a claim in order to avoid the difficulties resulting from the "Formstein-objection".

4. *Separate Patent as Defence in infringement proceedings*[15]

A similar problem arises in the following case: Again there is a prior patent and an infringing act or product. But now the infringing act itself is based on a patent. Does it have an effect on the question of infringement? Is the infringer prevented from being held to infringe any other patent, if he has a patent of his own? One the one side one may think: Yes, the granting of a patent tells me that the patented invention must be different enough from prior patents that it could not infringe them and the infringement court should be bound to that finding from the patent office. However the infringement court does not ask for differences between one patent and another but is comparing the elements of the patent claim with the elements of the accused act or product. If the accused act or product realizes all elements, literal infringement is established – whether separately patented or not.

The question whether the infringement court is bound to a patent granted to the alleged infringer is discussed only in regard to equivalent infringement. This

13 Cf. also E. Popp (*supra* note 11), at p. 321.

14 Cf. E. Popp (*supra* note 11), at p. 322.

15 For U.S. Law see U.S. Supreme Court, 56 U.S. 252, 271 (1853) - *Corning v. Burden*; Federal Circuit of 12 February 1996, 76 F.3d 1185, 37 U.S.P.Q.2d 1685, 1689 - *National Presto Indus. v. West Bend Co.*

is due to the fact, that – as already mentioned above - one precondition of equivalently use is obviousness to a person skilled in the art in the way that the same result that is achieved by the patent can be achieved by means of the modified element. If the patent office has granted a patent with respect to the modification of the prior patent due to inventiveness, it seems obvious that the infringement court is bound to that finding and cannot approve equivalent infringement. Because it may result in conflicting findings if the patent office is granting a patent due to inventiveness in view of a prior patent and the same patent than is to be found as infringing use of the prior patent in the infringement proceeding.

However on the other hand, the patent owner should not be deprived of an adequate reward if the variant is using important elements of the prior patent.[16] Therefore the objection of a separate patent is admissible and promising only if the reason of granting a patent to the modified element is evident from the grant proceeding.[17] The patent office has to make evident that the variant as a whole is inventive in view of the prior patent and is not only an inventive modification of the prior patent. Not only that such evidence is very rarely to be found,[18] but there is also a prevailing opinion that the patent as granted to the alleged infringer in any case has no binding effect and is just an expert opinion.[19]

5. *Revocation after a final and non-appealable judgement in the infringement proceedings*

But now a question not very difficult under German Patent Law:

What happens if there is a revocation of the patent after a final and non-appealable judgement in the infringement proceedings? In Germany there are three possibilities. First, the action to declare the execution out of the enforceable judgment inadmissible (Vollstreckungsabwehrklage - Sec. 767 German Code of Civil Procedure), second, the claim on account of unjust enrichment (Bereicherungsanspruch - Sec. 812 I German Civil Code) and third, the action for retrial of a case (Restitutionsklage - Sec. 580 No. 6 German Code of Civil Procedure by analogy). In all of these cases, objections against the enforceable claim are only admissible in so far as grounds upon which they are based could not

16 Cf. E. Körner, *Äquivalenz und abhängige Erfindung*, 2009 GRUR 97, 99; R. Kraßer (*supra* note 1), at p. 729.

17 Cf. E. Körner, *ibid.*

18 R. Kraßer (*supra* note 1), at p. 738.

19 Cf. R. König, *Patentverletzung durch erfinderische Abwandlung,* 1996 Mitt. 75, 81; P. Mes, *PatG*, 2nd ed. (2005), § 14 marginal note 81.

have been raised in the original proceeding.[20] And this is the fact because there is no such objection of invalidity in German infringement proceedings.[21]

But how is this handled in countries where judges have full power of judicial review? For example, in those countries an alleged infringer might be ordered to pay damages before the European Patent Office decides to revoke the patent at issue. Recently the Court of Appeals of England and Wales had to deal with such a case.[22] The appellants held, that it would be wrong if the one is entitled to receive, and the other is "obliged to pay, tens of millions of pounds for an infringement of a patent which, in light of its revocation, should never have been granted and, indeed, should be treated as if it had not ever been granted, including at the time of the alleged infringements. It would be wrong in principle, because damages would be awarded for infringement of a patent which *ex hypothesi* did not exist."[23] However the court did not agree. Although the revocation will put an end to an injunction granted in the earlier proceedings, "the issues determined in the first judgment in these proceedings, namely that the patent was valid and that the appellants did infringed it, are *res judicata* as between the parties."[24] As between the parties, therefore, the validity of the Patent is no more open to argument.[25] This means that a national court system can find a patent valid by a final and conclusive decision and yet later, in opposition proceedings it is determined that the same patent is invalid or must be reduced in scope. Again we see: To establish two separate proceedings will inevitably provoke risk of inconsistency.

6. *Patent Claim is irreproducible and incomprehensible*

And there is a further implication: What happens if the patent claim is absolutely not reproducible and does not make any sense and it is not possible to clarify the meaning of the claim at all?

20 Cf. Sec. 767 (2) German Code of Civil Procedure; R. Kraßer (*supra* note 1), at p. 892 et seq.

21 Cf. BGH 2006 GRUR 316 – *Koksofentür*; R. Kraßer (*supra* note 1), at p. 892 et seq.; K. Bacher, *Vernichtung des Patents nach rechtskräftigem Abschluss des Verletzungsprozesses*, 2009 GRUR 216, 217 et seq.

22 England and Wales Court of Appeal of 27 February 2004, 2004 EWCA Civ 213 - *Coflexip S.A. & Anor v Stolt Offshore Ms Ltd. & Ors*, available at http://www.bailii.org/ew/cases/EWCA/Civ/2004/213.html; see also decision of 25 April 2007, 2007 EWCA Civ 364 - *Unilin Beheer BV v Berry Floor NV & Ors*, available at http://www.bailii.org/ew/cases/EWCA/Civ/2007/364.html.

23 *Coflexip S.A. & Anor v Stolt Offshore Ms Ltd. & Ors* (*supra* note 22), at para. 26.

24 *Ibid.*, at para. 27.

25 *Ibidem.*

Recently the *German Federal Supreme Court* held that in such a case the infringement court cannot dismiss the infringement action only for those reasons but has to deal with the claim as specified in the patent.[26] It is quite obvious that this might be a thankless and an almost unaccomplishable task for the judges of the infringement court.

7. Criticism

Having given this short survey I will come to the concluding question: What are the arguments in favour of or against the dualism in German Patent Law and is it worth keeping or should we abolish it? On the one side, one might find the following con arguments: Duplication of workload, duplication of costs, risk of inconsistency, difficult and confusing questions and restrictions in defence (Over-Enforcement). Although the defendant could have filed an opposition or nullity action, it has to be considered, that defendants often are taken by surprise – particularly when they had no reason to expect a patent, granted notwithstanding the lack of novelty or inventiveness. But what are pro arguments? First and foremost one could say, that Courts are highly specialized and proceedings are more quickly.[27] But what about dogmatic reasons? It has been argued, that it would be strange, if for example a civil court had to deal with the effectiveness of the issuing of a driving licence in a civil proceeding concerning damages resulting from a traffic accident.[28] Such an example however does not apply to patent law. A driving licence does not prevent others from driving a car as well as a driving licence is not necessary in order to obtain damages. Instead it should be possible to integrate civil and administrative principles and peculiarities in one single procedure, as it is the case in other countries.

At the end of the day I think that the counterarguments are substantive and convincing but in a world where high-tech-innovations often become obsolesce in only two or three years, quickness and effectiveness of enforcement in Patent Litigation is of highest importance. Therefore it might be worth considering to abolish the dualism under German Patent Law, if it would be possible to maintain the current quickness and effectiveness of proceedings – for example by providing courts with an adequate number of highly educated judges.

26 BGH 2009 GRUR 653 – *road construction machine (Straßenbaumaschine)*.
27 *P. Mes* (*supra* note 2), at p. 411.
28 *P. Mes* (*supra* note 2), at p. 405.

List of Speakers and Authors

Professor Dr. habil. Michał du Vall

Holder of the Chair of Industrial Property Rights and Competition of the Intellectual Property Law Institute at the Jagiellonian University, Vice-Rector of the Jagiellonian University Kraków

Professor Dr. iur. habil. Horst-Peter Götting, LL.M. (London)

Holder of the Chair for Civil Law with special emphasis on Industrial Property and Copyright Law; Director of the Institute for Intellectual Property, Competition and Media Law (IGEWeM) at the Technische Universität Dresden; Honorary Professor at the University of Leipzig; Judge at the Oberlandesgericht (Higher Regional Court) Dresden

Ass. iur. Philipp Hanske, LL.M., (Aberdeen)

Assistant and lecturer at the Institute for Intellectual Property, Competition and Media Law (IGEWeM) at the Technische Universität Dresden

Ass. iur. Sven Hetmank

Assistant and lecturer at the Institute for Intellectual Property, Competition and Media Law (IGEWeM) at the Technische Universität Dresden

Dr. Dariusz Kasprzycki

Assistant and lecturer at the Institute of Intellectual Property Law, Jagiellonian University Kraków

Ass. iur. Rüdiger Müller

Candidate notary with the Saxon Chamber of Civil Law Notaries, former assistant and lecturer at the Institute for Intellectual Property, Competition and Media Law (IGEWeM) at the Technische Universität Dresden

Dr. Justyna Ożegalska-Trybalska

Assistant and lecturer at the Institute of Intellectual Property Law, Jagiellonian University Kraków

Heike Röder-Hitschke, LL.M. (Dresden/Strasbourg)

Lawyer and certified specialist for Intellectual Property, Kaye Scholer LLP, Frankfurt am Main; Member of the Institute for Intellectual Property, Competition and Media Law (IGEWeM) at the Technische Universität Dresden

Dr. Sybilla Stanisławska-Kloc

Assistant and lecturer at the Institute of Intellectual Property Law, Jagiellonian University Kraków

Dr. Tomasz Targosz

Assistant and lecturer at the Institute of Intellectual Property Law, Jagiellonian University Kraków

Dr. Anna Tischner

Assistant and lecturer at the Institute of Intellectual Property Law, Jagiellonian University Kraków